ACTS
devotional journal

Journey in the Word Study Series

The Book of
ACTS

The People, Miracles and Message God Used
to Turn the World Upside Down

Dr. Craig Hamlin

515 Flower St, Los Angeles, CA 90071, United States
213.995.3059
www.amzprohub.com

Copyright © 2023 by Dr. Craig Hamlin
All rights reserved.

The author has taken great care in researching, writing, and preparing this book and has based the content on a variety of primary and secondary sources. Consequently, the accuracy of much of the content depends on the accuracy of these sources. Moreover, the author has given credit to other authors and sources to the best of his ability and does not claim to have written the content that is cited as his own and does not claim liability for its use. The photos and charts in the book are not cited in the text but are cited in the end notes for enhanced readability of the text.

Paperback ISBN - 978-1-960757-56-2
Hardcover ISBN - 978-1-960757-57-9

DEDICATION

This book is dedicated to my wife, Jenny, who has always encouraged me and believed in me!

With all my love...

CONTENTS

Foreword		1
Introduction to The Book of Acts		5
Outline of The Book of Acts		7

1	What Now? Waiting with Purpose *Acts 1:1-26*	10	
2	The Promise Fulfilled *Acts 2:1-47*		14
3	The Wonder of a Miracle *Acts 3:1-26*	18	
4	No Other Name *Acts 4:1-37*	22	
5	The Unstoppable Church *Acts 5:1-42*	26	
6	Growing Pains *Acts 6:1-15*		30
7	Preaching the Old Testament *Acts 7:1-60*		34
8	A Faith that is Alive *Acts 8:1-40*	38	
9	New Life in Christ *Acts 9:1-43*	42	
10	Our Mission is Everyone! *Acts 10:1-48*	46	

11	A Heart Like His *Acts 11:1-30*	50
12	The Storm Before the Calm *Acts 12:1-25*	54
13	Sent Out *Acts 13:1-52*	58
14	Living for the Glory of One *Acts 14:1-28*	62
15	Solo Fide! *Acts 15:1-41*	66
16	The Miracle at Midnight *Acts 16:1-40*	70
17	Turning the World Upside Down *Acts 17:1-34*	74
18	Press On Under Pressure *Acts 18:1-28*	78
19	From Darkness to His Glorious Light *Acts 19:1-41*	82
20	Never Stop Being an Encourager *Acts 20:1-38*	86
21	The Importance of Friendship *Acts 21:1-26*	90
22	Every Christian Has a Testimony *Acts 21:27-22:29*	94
23	Never Give Up! *Acts 22:30-23:35*	98

24	On Trial for the Gospel *Acts 24:1-27*	102
25	Trusting the Purpose and Plan of God *Acts 25:1-27*	106
26	Here I Stand! *Acts 26:1-32*	110
27	No Storm is Too Strong *Acts 27:1-44*	114
28	The Rest of the Story *Acts 28:1-31*	118
References		123
About the Author		125

FOREWORD

God created you for relationship.

There is no doubt as you read the bible that God made you to know Him personally. The very thought of this should amaze you and humble you. God, who created all things, wants you to know Him deeply. The bible is the story of God's rescue of humanity from their choice to rebel against their Creator and the condemnation that choice demanded. The bible tells the story of God's extraordinary love for every person, coming to rebellious humanity and offering them forgiveness and a relationship with Him now and for eternity.

The bible is an extraordinary book that is history's most amazing book, written by 40 different authors over 1,500 years by kings, peasants, fishermen, philosophers, poets, and scholars on three continents and in three different languages. It has been read by more people and printed in more languages than any other book in human history. For Christian spiritual growth, it is an essential discipline. To read the bible prayerfully and thoughtfully is the key to clearly hearing the voice of God and discerning how to make wise decisions. The goal of this devotional-style journal is to help you study the bible more enjoyably, but it's also to give you a deeper love for God's word. The more you love God's word, the more you will fall in the love with the Author of this word. The bible has been described as a love letter to those who love Him. Love letters are words written down for someone of significance to read but also for the recipient to reciprocate the love being expressed. That is why this is not just a devotional but a journal as well.

Writing down your thoughts helps you discover the truth and really grasp its meaning. Journaling also helps you think through ways to apply it, memorize passages, and keep a timeline of your journey with the Lord. Journaling may be difficult for you, as it is with many people, but if you try, you might discover that the rewards are transformative.

For me, journaling has been a journey of inconsistency. I would come across a person who loved to journal and get inspired, but within a week, I had either lost it or put it aside. I never could figure out how to really put my thoughts down or follow a Bible study method that would stick and help me stay consistent. Around 2012, I picked up a book called *Real Life Discipleship* by Jim Putman. The book articulated what God had been speaking into my heart about discipleship and disciple-making. I attended a conference centered around the book, and through a series of relationships built at the conference, I began picking up techniques people were using to journal their thoughts during their quiet time.

After a few years of adapting several different methods to my own way of thinking and working through scripture, I came up with **GRASP**. The main inspiration for **GRASP** came from my introduction to the Discovery Bible Study method, or DBS. This bible study method has been and continues to be used around the world in personal devotional studies and small group studies. Thousands of churches have been planted, and millions of lives changed through this approach to scripture. DBS changed the way I did bible study, and I hope my adaptation of it for journaling and study will help you, as well.

The devotional-style journal is laid out simply, giving you a guideline for what to write. The acronym **GRASP** is all you need to help you stay on track and write down your thoughts daily. **GRASP** is a way to ask five questions:

1. What **GRABBED** my attention?
2. What did I **REALIZE** about God and people?
3. How can I **APPLY** this passage?
4. How will I **SPECIFICALLY** apply it this week?
5. Who is one **PERSON** with whom I can share what I've learned?

In addition to using GRASP, there is a section for prayer, scripture memory, thanksgiving and some thoughts to share if you are doing this with a small group.

Let's look a little closer at how to use GRASP:

G – What Grabbed My Attention?

When you read a passage of Scripture, read the text with expectation. What stands out or jumps out at you? What confused you or challenged you? It could be an action, a principle, a command, or a truth claim. Write that verse or verses down, and then write why that Scripture grabbed your attention. This may lead you toward your application as well.

R – What did I Realize about God and people?

The bible is the story of God relating to man and man relating to God and their fellow man. Every time you read a passage, look for what is said about God's **character** or how God **works** in the passage. Look for what God says or what is said about God.

The contrast is people. How are people portrayed? How do they respond in the passage? Stick to the passage without interpretation. What is in the text? Write down the facts.

A – How could I Apply this Scripture?

One of the most difficult sections but revealing is the application. Sometimes it is hard to find the ways a text can be applied. Application is basically how we adjust to God or align our character and conduct to His. Basically, we are looking at what we realized about ourselves or others in light of the character and conduct of God. We make adjustments to Him. He does not make adjustments to us. Here are questions that can help you think through how to apply the Scripture:

- *Is there a sin to avoid?*
- *Is there a command to obey?*
- *Is there a promise to claim?*
- *Is there an example to follow?*
- *Is there a truth to know?*

S – How will I Specifically apply the truth this week?

This is where your time with the Lord gets real. It's one thing to think about ways to apply the text, but another to commit to an action step during the week. Writing an "I will" statement is a commitment to being a doer of the Word (James 1:22). While writing this statement is a good first step, to be most effective, you need to share this statement with someone who has permission to ask you how it went during the week. Accountability is critical for spiritual growth because we all tend to live in the lower expectations. Write out your "I will" statement in a **SMART** way. In other words, the statement needs to be: *Specific, Measurable, Attainable, Realistic, and Timely.*

Example: I will speak more kindly to my wife this week and ask her on Friday how I have shown her kindness with my words.

P – Who is one Person with whom you can share?

Nothing solidifies truth in us like application and proclamation. Who is one person with whom you could share what you learned for the day or week? While your spouse or friend are natural people with whom you like to share, try sharing with people who need encouragement or need to hear the Gospel. Share the story or principles naturally as if over a cup of coffee. God will use His word to accomplish great things! Don't keep it to yourself!

Dr. Craig Hamlin
Enjoy the Journey!

Introduction to the Book of Acts

The Book of Acts is the continuation of Luke's gospel written to Theophilus about the life of Jesus. Luke was not a disciple of Jesus but a convert to Christianity and partner in ministry with the Apostle Paul. Luke was a physician and meticulously searched for details from sources such as Peter and Mary, the mother of Jesus, to get the specific details of Jesus' life and ministry. He would do the same in this account that detailed the birth of the Church, the ministry of Peter, and the ministry of Paul.

The Book of Acts is called, The Acts of the Apostles because it traces the steps of those who had been with Jesus, or in Paul's case, one with whom Jesus had appeared (Acts 9). By chapter 13, Luke moves exclusively to the journeys of Paul as he recruits several partners in ministry to accompany him on three different missionary journeys West into modern-day Turkey (Asia Minor) and Greece, where Paul planted churches and preached the Gospel.

Hans Conzelmann notes that since Luke authored the work, it is reasonable to date Acts between 60 and 100 AD. However, if we wanted a precise date, you should reason that at the end of Acts, Luke does not give the details of what happened to Paul awaiting judgment in Rome. Therefore, if Luke did not provide those details because they had not happened at the completion of the book, the date for Acts would be 62 or 63 AD. We do not know much about the recipient of Acts, Theophilus, except that Luke refers to him in his gospel account as "most excellent" Theophilus (Luke 1:3). In the New Testament, that designation was always reserved for a governing official.

The book's purpose is clear: to give an account of the events after the resurrection and ascension of Jesus Christ by His apostles and to explain the birth of the Church after Pentecost as the Holy Spirit began to move into the hearts of people, both Jew and Gentile. The primary emphasis for Luke was the spread of the Gospel in

Jerusalem, Judea, Samaria, and the nations. Luke shows the difficulties faced by the new church (6 and 15), the formulas for the church's ministry (2:42-47), and the moments of incredible miracles throughout the book. Luke also gives us a clear picture of the difficulties faced by Peter and Paul. They were imprisoned, stoned, and persecuted consistently, but through it all, they persevered for the sake of the gospel to the nations.

The Book of Acts is a fast-moving and engaging story of triumph and trials, revealing the power of the Gospel and God's heart for every race, tribe, and nation. The book reads like a novel but is packed with relevant truths that can be applied easily to everyday life. Michael Morrison of Grace Communion International wrote:

"The Book of Acts may be read for history, and it may also be read to strengthen our faith and commitment to Jesus Christ. As we read, we can put ourselves in the apostles' sandals, to feel their boldness in preaching the gospel and their fears when facing persecution. We can marvel that the apostles, right after being flogged, were "rejoicing because they had been counted worthy of suffering disgrace for the Name [of Jesus]" (Acts 5:41). And by reading about their faith and perseverance, we can be a little more emboldened to face our own crises with the help of the same Holy Spirit."

Nothing can bless you more than reading and applying the Word of God. As you read the Book of Acts, enjoy what the Lord shows you and be blessed by the fruit God places in your life as you obey Him. Historical narratives are sometimes hard to apply, but when you look at how God is presented in the story, His character, His conduct, and how He moved among the people, you can see how it contrasts your own character or conduct. As you pray, look for ways to adjust your own life so that your character and conduct match the immutable nature of God.

OUTLINE of ACTS

I.	Introduction	1:1-5
II.	**The Ascension and Commission**	**1:6-11**
	Jesus' Commission	1:6-8
	Jesus' Ascension	1:9-11
III.	**The Holy Spirit Ascends**	**1:12-2:47**
	Disciples Gather for Prayer	1:12-26
	The Holy Spirit Arrives	2:1-13
	Peter's Sermon	2:14-41
	The Church Begins	2:42-27
IV.	**The Church in Jerusalem**	**3:1-8:3**
	Healing and Peter's Second Sermon	3:1-26
	Persecution and the Church's Prayer	4:1-37
	Lying to the Holy Spirit	5:1-11
	More Persecution and Courage	5:12-42
	First Major Challenge	6:1-7
	Stephen's Sermon and Martyrdom	6:8-7:60
	Saul Persecutes the Church	8:1-3
V.	**The Church in Judea and Samaria**	**8:4-12:25**
	The Gospel to the Samaritans	8:4-25
	Phillip and the Ethiopian Eunuch	8:26-40
	Saul's Conversion and Early Life	9:1-31

	Miracles of Healing by Peter	9:32-43
	Peter's Vision & Witness in Caesarea	10:1-48
	Barnabas and Saul in Antioch/Judea	11:1-30
	Persecutions Heat Up	12:1-25

VI. **The Church Sent Out to the Nations 13:1-28:31**
  Barnabas and Saul Sent Out 13:1-14:28
  The Jerusalem Council   15:1-35
  Paul and Barnabas Diverge   15:36-41
  Timothy, Paul and Silas   16:1-5
  The Macedonian Call   16:6-10
  Lydia's Conversion   16:11-15
  Paul's Witness in Prison   16:16-40
  Thessalonica   17:1-15
  Athens   17:16-34
  Corinth   18:1-17
  Antioch   18:18-23
  Apollos in Ephesus   18:24-28
  Paul in Ephesus   19:1-41
  Paul in Macedonia   20:1-16
  Paul with the Ephesians   20:17-38
  Paul's Return in Jerusalem   21:1-22:29

VII. **Paul Defenses Before Authorities   22:3026:32**
  Paul Before the Council   22:30-23:11
  Plot to Kill Paul   23:12-22
  Paul Before Felix   23:24-24:27
  Paul Appeals to Caesar   25:1-12
  Paul's Before Agrippa   25:13-26:32

VIII.	Paul Sails for Rome	27:1-28:31
	Paul is Shipwrecked	27:1-44
	Paul on Malta	28:1-10
	Paul Arrives in Rome	28:11-16
	Paul's Ministry in Rome	28:17-31

The Acts of the Apostles is the most lyrical of books. Live in that book, I exhort you; it is a tonic, the greatest tonic I know of in the realm of the Spirit."

~ D. Martyn Lloyd-Jones

1

Acts 1:1-26

What Now? Waiting with Purpose

Have you ever been in a place in your life where one significant part has ended or changed and now you are asking yourself, "What do I do now?" Every parent has this feeling when they bring their first child home from the hospital and then they have it again when they are empty-nesters. The disciples were going through a moment like that after they had been with Jesus for 40 days after His crucifixion and resurrection. Jesus ascended into the clouds, and after that moment, they must have looked around in the quietness of the moment and said, "What are we going to do now?"

Jesus had been with His disciples, at least the main twelve, for over three years, night and day, pouring into their lives and preparing for this moment. He had already promised them that He would never leave them, and He promised to send a Helper (John 14). Jesus had told them that their mission was to make disciples of all nations, but when the moment came, they hesitated. One of their own had turned his back on them and betrayed Jesus. At the same time, Jesus had appeared to them and gave them and told that "you will receive power when the Holy Spirit has come upon you, and you will be My witnesses in Jerusalem, Judea, Samaria and to the end of the earth" (Acts 1:8).

Talk about being in a pressure-packed moment! The disciples were coming off three and a half years of intense ministry among fickle people, only to lose Judas and now faced with a mission to take Jesus' message to every part of the world.

What would they do? How would they handle this mission and this pressure? How would any of us? Maybe we get reactionary and forge ahead without thinking about the consequences. Maybe we crawl up in a ball with a full-blown panic attack. What the disciples did helps us. They did what they knew to do, find a legitimate replacement for Judas, and then do what Jesus told them to do: Wait!

Waiting is not always seen as a way to fulfill our purpose, but when we wait on the Lord, He works with us and through us to do things in a way that doesn't create more problems. Waiting on the Lord is about allowing the Spirit of God to respond in his timing, to utilize His wisdom and do what He says as He says it. G. Campbell Morgan once said, "Waiting for God is not laziness. Waiting for God is not going to sleep. Waiting for God is not the abandonment of effort. Waiting for God means, first, activity under command; second, readiness for any new command that may come; third, the ability to do nothing until the command is given."

What now? It's a great question, but it's a question that is filled with anticipation for what God is about to do and a moment of discipline to help you know you can trust the Lord. So, today, as you wait on the Lord, know that your ultimate purpose has not changed, "go and make disciples of all nations", but realize that any disruptions in your day or crisis that may arise, it's an opportunity for you to wait with purpose.

G. Campbell Morgan said, "Waiting for God is not laziness. Waiting for God is not going to sleep. Waiting for God is not the abandonment of effort. Waiting for God means, first, activity under command; second, readiness for any new command that may come; third, the ability to do nothing until the command is given."

Read Acts 1:1-26   Date: Oct 16

GRASP
BIBLE JOURNAL PERSONAL NOTES

G   What **Grabbed** your attention, confused you or stood out?

R   What did you **Realize** about God and the people in this passage?

God?

People?

A   How could you **Apply** this to your life?

> *Is there a sin to avoid?*
> *Is there a command to obey?*
> *Is there a promise to claim?*
> *Is there an example to follow?*
> *Is there a truth to know?*

S   What is one **Specific** thing you could do this week to apply the truth from this passage? Write out "I will…".

P   Write a **Prayer** of commitment to the Lord.

What are you **Thankful** for today?

Write out a verse from this chapter to **Memorize** this week:

"If you have a strong purpose in life, you don't have to be pushed. Your passion will drive you there."
~ Roy T. Bennett

2

Acts 2:1-47

The Promise Fulfilled

Dwight L. Moody was a shoe salesman from Chicago who fell in love with Jesus and started sharing his faith with everyone he met. Even though he was never ordained or had formal training, God used him to reach thousands for Christ as an evangelist. There was a group of British pastors who were planning a crusade and the name of D. L.

Moody came up as a possible preacher. One British pastor said with skepticism: "Why do we need this Mr. Moody? He's unordained, uneducated, and inexperienced. Who does he think he is? Does he think he has a monopoly on the Holy Spirit?"

But another, wiser pastor, who had heard D.L. Moody preach responded, "Mr. Moody doesn't have a monopoly on the Holy Spirit, but the Holy Spirit has a monopoly on Mr. Moody."

When Jesus was wrapping up His earthly ministry, His disciples became a bit distraught. They had followed Him and now realized that He was leaving. What would become of them? Would they also be crucified? Would they have the courage to tell anyone about what Jesus had done? Earlier, Jesus had told them that He would not leave them as orphans, but the Helper, the Holy Spirit, would come and teach them and be their peace (John 14).

Then, as Jesus was leaving, He promised them that if they would wait, they would receive power from the Holy Spirit to help them fulfill their mission of being His ambassador to the nations. As Acts 2 opens, they are waiting. Then comes Pentecost! Author and pastor Tony Merida writes that Pentecost means the prophecy has been fulfilled, the last days have dawned, everyone can know God intimately, and that Christ ascended to the throne (Acts 2:14-36). Pentecost marked one of the three major feasts in Israel's calendar. It was the 15th (pentekoste) day after Passover.

Why is this significant? The events of the cross, the resurrection, and Pentecost are connected and help to see how God's redemptive plan included not only Christ's death for us but His continued presence in our lives, guiding, directing, convicting, and empowering us! Our Lord was and is the Promise-Keeper!! The promise He made in the garden to forever deal with sin, He fulfilled through His death and resurrection. He fulfilled his promise to never leave us when He sent His Spirit into our hearts. He is our presence!

Now, Peter's sermon mixed Old Testament prophecy and New Testament reality into a beautiful array of truth that meant that every person who believed would be forgiven of all their sin and receive the Holy Spirit. This would not be according to their goodness or ability but according to His grace. "For the promise is for you and your children and for all who are afar off, everyone whom the Lord our God calls to Himself" (2:39). With that, the Church was born with over 3,000 souls coming to faith in Christ. They met, they prayed, they taught, they remembered, they communed, they served, and they worshipped. "And the Lord added to their number daily those who were being saved" (2:47). The Holy Spirit's coming on Pentecost meant we could forever trust the Lord. We do not have to lean on our own understanding, but always know that wherever He leads us, whatever He allows in our lives, He will always be there to walk us through and empower us to be His voice in this world. The disciples were about to enter a faith journey where they would need to trust in the Lord. He had their back! He has yours, too!

Read Acts 2:1-47   Date: _____

GRASP
BIBLE JOURNAL PERSONAL NOTES

G   What **Grabbed** your attention, confused you or stood out?

R   What did you **Realize** about God and the people in this passage?

God?

People?

A   How could you **Apply** this to your life?

> *Is there a sin to avoid?*
> *Is there a command to obey?*
> *Is there a promise to claim?*
> *Is there an example to follow?*
> *Is there a truth to know?*

S   What is one **Specific** thing you could do this week to apply the truth from this passage? Write out "I will…".

P   Write a **Prayer** of commitment to the Lord.

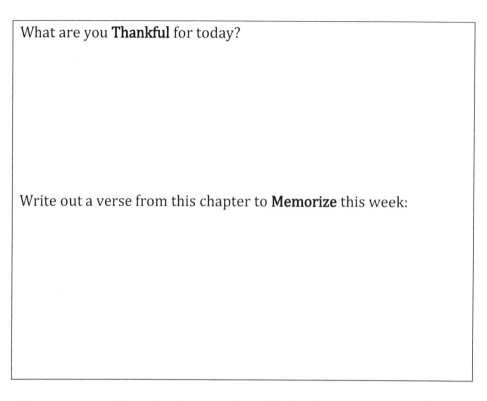

"Peace comes not from the absence of trouble, but from the presence of God."
~ *Alexander MacClaren*

3

Acts 3:1-26

The Wonder of a Miracle

Ray Stedman, in his classic book, Authentic Christianity, writes, "An alcoholic became a believer, was asked how he could possibly believe all the nonsense in the Bible about miracles. "You don't believe that Jesus changed the water into wine do you?" "I sure do, because in our house Jesus changed the whiskey into furniture."

The Church had been birthed, and people were coming to faith in Christ! The Holy Spirit was dwelling in the souls of every believer, and God was doing the miraculous! Miracles ... the most mysterious of life's events. Unexplained, awe-inspiring, wonderful, and terrifying all at the same time. Peter and John entered the temple at 3 pm for prayer. Just as Jesus met a blind man, now they saw a man who could not see them, but sensed they are there. The only thing he knew to do was ask for money. He had been doing that all his life.

Miracles were rare; beggars were not. On every street corner, and especially in front of the temple, you would find someone trying to survive, hoping that some good soul would give them a shekel. Peter and John had no money to give, but what they did have was far more valuable. Peter looked at the man and said, "Silver and gold, have I none, but what I do have I give to you. In the name of Jesus Christ of Nazareth, rise up and walk!"

The lame man was raised up and immediately found strength in his feet and began to leap around, praising God. Wouldn't you? Miracles are those kinds of supernatural events that take your breath away. In the early Church, before the scriptures were entirely written, the skepticism of people leaned away from God to the idols of the land. The Lord used miracles to grab people's attention and cause them to listen to the message. Miracles can be seen in scripture as (1) Directional: people praised the Lord! (2) Healing: God restored a body or life; (3) Hope: the miracle gave hopeless people hope that God was there; (4) Community: those who received the miracle rejoined their community and encouraged others; and (5) Conviction: Miracles always lead to greater, firmer faith.

People gathered, as you could imagine, to get a glimpse of this all-too-familiar crippled man completely healed! Peter, like any good pastor, seized the moment and began to preach the gospel. "Repent therefore, and turn back, that your sins may be blotted out ...". That was it!

God healed this man for others to hear about Jesus Christ. God will use any means necessary to get others to consider Him. Think about everything He has done to get faith into your heart. Think about the generations, the choices people made, the people He put in your life, and the circumstances that had to happen in perfect harmony even though you thought mistakes were being made. God was working through it all. Thank Him today for the miracle that is your life in Christ. YOU are a miracle!

Read Acts 3:1-26   Date: _____

GRASP
BIBLE JOURNAL PERSONAL NOTES

G   What **Grabbed** your attention, confused you or stood out?

R   What did you **Realize** about God and the people in this passage?

God?

People?

A   How could you **Apply** this to your life?

> *Is there a sin to avoid?*
> *Is there a command to obey?*
> *Is there a promise to claim?*
> *Is there an example to follow?*
> *Is there a truth to know?*

S   What is one **Specific** thing you could do this week to apply the truth from this passage? Write out "I will…".

P Write a **Prayer** of commitment to the Lord.

What are you **Thankful** for today?

Write out a verse from this chapter to **Memorize** this week:

"Miracles are a retelling in small letters of the very same story which is written across the whole world in letters too large for some of us to see."
~ *C.S. Lewis*

4

Acts 4:1-37

No Other Name

There is nothing more frustrating to our enemy, Satan, than a miracle from Jesus and the message of Jesus! After the miracle, the opposition launched its threats and the first wave of persecution began to sweep through Jerusalem. "By what power or by what name did you do this?" That was the question! The religious leaders didn't want to know the real answer because they thought they had rid themselves of the One who was getting credit for so many "mysterious" things happening over the last few years.

When Peter was faced with answering this question, however, he had only one response – "This Jesus, whom you crucified, is the stone that was rejected by you, the builders, which has become the cornerstone. And there is salvation is no one else, for there is **no other name** under heaven given among men by which we must be saved." Talk about boldness! Bring it, Peter!

Probably the greatest compliment Peter (and any Christian, for that matter) could have received was given in Acts 4:13 "And they recognized that they had been with Jesus." That is what every Christian should want from their life ... for Jesus to rub off on us so much that we clearly reek of Jesus!

When Peter made that stand, here's what happened: God gave them all clarity in their message and boldness to share it (4:19). Then, when the people of God prayed, the Lord shook the place, and they were all filled with the Holy Spirit (4:23-31). Finally, the Church grew even stronger as great grace was upon them all (4:32-37). Our lives are significantly changed when we live and speak in the name of Jesus. Then, when the Holy Spirit works in and through us, our love and generosity are transformed, and we see God do things that only God can do! This is the power of our God!

A young boy traveling by airplane to visit his grandparents sat beside a man who happened to be a seminary professor. The boy was reading a Sunday school take-home paper when the professor thought he would have some fun with the boy. "Young man," said the professor, "If you can tell me something God can do, I"ll give you a big, shiny apple." The boy thought for a moment and then replied, "Mister, if you can tell me something God can't do, I"ll give you a whole barrel of apples!"

God's power to heal a disease, open blinded eyes or remove a demon paled in comparison to His power to transform a life through the indwelling of the Holy Spirit. That is the resurrection power that Peter used to preach the Gospel and it is the power that is given to you to be His hands and feet.

Read Acts 4:1-37   Date: _____

GRASP
BIBLE JOURNAL PERSONAL NOTES

G   What **Grabbed** your attention, confused you or stood out?

R   What did you **Realize** about God and the people in this passage?

God?

People?

A   How could you **Apply** this to your life?

> Is there a sin to avoid?
> Is there a command to obey?
> Is there a promise to claim?
> Is there an example to follow?
> Is there a truth to know?

S What is one **Specific** thing you could do this week to apply the truth from this passage? Write out "I will…".

P Write a **Prayer** of commitment to the Lord.

What are you **Thankful** for today?

Write out a verse from this chapter to **Memorize** this week:

"The greatest weapon we have against evil is doing good in Jesus's name."
~ Kay Warren

5
Acts 5:1-42

The Unstoppable Church

Kirk Cameron once said, "God steps into the suffering with us, and He takes it on himself, and He walks through it with us, and He uses it to create something in you that is unstoppable." Those words are a great description of what God did to create the Church. He stepped into our suffering, took our sin on Himself, empowered us with the Holy Spirit, and created the unstoppable Church!

As the young church in Jerusalem worked to minister to the people coming to Christ, many of whom were losing their families, possessions, and freedoms, God used an incident that shook the church (5:1-11). Ananias and Sapphira got in on the missions giving offerings, but their pledges were halfhearted and deceitful. Already, the enemy was trying to stop the church in its tracks, and the old nature that can plague a church marred a beautiful beginning. It's amazing how sin can creep into a church, into our lives, and grieve the Holy Spirit. We must guard against it with a passionate desire to treasure Christ above all else.

From the incredible display of God's holy righteousness, we see the power of God miraculously healing people. Nothing in all of Jerusalem and the surrounding areas gained more attention than the stir Peter and the apostles were making. The religious leaders knew they had to stop this thing before it got out of hand, but what they didn't count on was that the church is unstoppable because the church was birthed by an unstoppable God!

As you read through the account of the apostle's arrest and imprisonment, you are struck with the boldness and conviction they showed as they stated, "We must obey God rather than men." The lone religious leader who had any sense about the matter was a respected man named Gamaliel. His words help us describe the nature of the unstoppable church: "If this plan or this undertaking is of man, it will fail, but if it is of God, you will not be able to overthrow it" (5:38-39).

The Church, God's holy people, the body of Christ, is an unstoppable force of truth and grace, and you are a member of it! In his classic book, *The Body*, Chuck Colson writes, "Yet membership in a confessing body is fundamental to the faithful Christian life. Failure to do so defies the explicit warning not to forsake "our assembling together." His understanding of this prompted Martin Luther to say, "Apart from the church, salvation is impossible." Not that the church provides salvation; God does. But because the "saved" one can't fulfill what it means to be a Christian apart from the church, membership becomes the indispensable mark of salvation." John Calvin also writes, "So highly does the Lord esteem the communion of His church that He considers everyone a traitor and apostate from religion who perversely withdraws himself from any Christian society which preserves the true ministry of the word and sacraments."

Being a part of the church is not being a part of a social club or an option for Christians that can take-it or leave-it. The Church is God's plan for every believer to get the context of the Gospel, build a community of committed people and be a force of love and service to the world. Be someone who genuinely longs to contribute and learn from others who are not perfect but who are all drawn to the love of Christ.

Read Acts 5:1-42   Date: _____

GRASP
BIBLE JOURNAL PERSONAL NOTES

G What **Grabbed** your attention, confused you or stood out?

R What did you **Realize** about God and the people in this passage?

God?

People?

A How could you **Apply** this to your life?

> *Is there a sin to avoid?*
> *Is there a command to obey?*
> *Is there a promise to claim?*
> *Is there an example to follow?*
> *Is there a truth to know?*

S   What is one **Specific** thing you could do this week to apply the truth from this passage? Write out "I will…".

P   Write a **Prayer** of commitment to the Lord.

What are you **Thankful** for today?

Write out a verse from this chapter to **Memorize** this week:

> "Every believer is part of the church and every church is a part of the unstoppable mission to make disciples of the nations."
> ~ Jason Williams

6

Acts 6:1-15

Growing Pains

What would it be like to grow from 6'2" to 6'10" in 18 months? That is what happened to NBA All-Star Anthony Davis in high school between the end of his sophomore year and senior year. Davis entered high school as an outstanding guard with a college ready to recruit him, but by the end of high school, he was the number one high school player in the nation, eventually playing for Kentucky and then the famed L.A. Lakers.

Growing pains are often a hassle for many. We have all gone through them to some degree. They can either cause us to be frustratingly discouraged or spur us toward glory. In Acts 6, the early church had some growing pains. The apostles were trying to do all the ministry and lead the Christians through prayer and preaching. At that moment, a choice was made concerning priorities, not in the area of what an apostle would do, but what place prayer and preaching would take alongside acts of kindness and love.

No one doubted that acts of love were important. No one would say that feeding the hungry, finding homes for the homeless, or ministering to orphans and widows were unimportant things. However, the early church decided that if they neglected prayer and preaching, soon there would be no one to serve the hungry, homeless, or hurt. Why? Because love for God and love for people happened through transformed lives, and only through the gospel could they truly discover and live out the love of Jesus Christ.

Therefore, the church leaders opened the door for everyone to work together and serve, using their skills, calling, gifts and passions. One of those chosen that day was a Spirit-filled man named Stephen. No man in the New Testament resembled Jesus more than Stephen. He was full of grace and power. Stephen spoke with wisdom and the Spirit. He baffled the crowds and frustrated religious leaders. Like Jesus, Stephen was arrested unjustly, lied about, and later put to death without a real trial.

When the emperor Valens threatened Eusebuis with confiscation of all his goods, torture, banishment, or even death, the courageous Christian replied, "He needs not fear confiscation, who has nothing to lose; nor banishment, to whom heaven is his country; nor torments, when his body can be destroyed at one blow; nor death, which is the only way to set him at liberty from sin and sorrow."

Godly men and women are often borne out of crisis to lead with courage and conviction. They can sit under accusation, be lied about and scorned, and yet, in their presence, their face shines like angels. May God use us to be uniters, not dividers ... bold, not weak ... proclaimers, not silent. Let the growing pains of faith not slow you down, but be the catalyst to greater ministry in your life.

Read Acts 6:1-15   Date: _____

GRASP
BIBLE JOURNAL PERSONAL NOTES

G   What **Grabbed** your attention, confused you or stood out?

R   What did you **Realize** about God and the people in this passage?

God?

People?

A   How could you **Apply** this to your life?

> *Is there a sin to avoid?*
> *Is there a command to obey?*
> *Is there a promise to claim?*
> *Is there an example to follow?*
> *Is there a truth to know?*

S   What is one **Specific** thing you could do this week to apply the truth from this passage? Write out "I will…".

P   Write a **Prayer** of commitment to the Lord.

What are you **Thankful** for today?

Write out a verse from this chapter to **Memorize** this week:

"True Christ likeness, true companionship with Christ, comes at the point where it is hard not to respond as he would."
~ Dallas Willard

Acts 7:1-60

Preaching the Old Testament

Hudson Taylor found the China Inland Mission and gave his life to get the gospel to people in China. With so many obstacles in his path, he understood the faithfulness of God to provide in ways no one could see coming. He wrote in his journal: "Our heavenly Father is a very experienced One. He knows very well that His children wake up with a good appetite every morning...He sustained 3 million Israelites in the wilderness for 40 years. We do not expect He will send 3 million missionaries to China; but if He did, He would have ample means to sustain them all...Depend on it, God's work done in God's way will never lack God's supply."

Writer and Old Testament scholar Scott Gibson wrote, "The Old Testament was the Bible of our Savior, the apostles, and the early church. We cannot understand them or their work if we ignore the fount from which they drank or the authoritative library from which they read."

Stephen had been accused of blasphemy, and then in a divine, sovereign moment, the high priest asked him if what people had said about him was true. Without PowerPoint slides, an iPad, or note cards, Stephen recited the Old Testament from Genesis 12 to 1 Kings, from Abraham to Solomon, and then to Jesus! While the sermon was a great history lesson through Genesis, mainly Stephen's point was the faithfulness of God.

This is the message of the Bible. God is faithful! Stephen showed it as God chose Abraham to lead a people to an unknown land out of paganism and into monotheism. Out of devotion to the gods of man's imagination, to an unwavering devotion to the Only True God, he recounted the lives of Isaac, Jacob, and Joseph. He mentioned some specifics along the way and then moved toward Israel's great savior, Moses. God's faithfulness to the promise He made with Abraham was the common thread, which Moses picked up as he was directed by God to deliver enslaved Israel from Egypt.

Stephen quickly made his way through time to David and then to Solomon. He wanted to move the conversation to the temple. Stephen was accused of speaking words against the temple and saying that Jesus would turn their worship on its head. He jolted them when he called them stiff-necked people, betrayers, and murderers. The truth hurt, but the truth was what they needed and - oh yes - what we need!

If one thing is clear from the Old Testament, it is that God is serious about sin but merciful to those who repent. Enraged, the people stoned Stephen as he looked into heaven, saw Jesus, and just as His Savior had done from the cross, Stephen cried out, "Lord, do not hold this sin against them." That's the power of the Gospel preached, believed, and lived. Now, GO and do likewise!

Read Acts 7:1-60   Date: _____

GRASP
BIBLE JOURNAL PERSONAL NOTES

G   What **Grabbed** your attention, confused you or stood out?

R   What did you **Realize** about God and the people in this passage?

God?

People?

A   How could you **Apply** this to your life?

> *Is there a sin to avoid?*
> *Is there a command to obey?*
> *Is there a promise to claim?*
> *Is there an example to follow?*
> *Is there a truth to know?*

S   What is one **Specific** thing you could do this week to apply the truth from this passage? Write out "I will…".

P   Write a **Prayer** of commitment to the Lord.

What are you **Thankful** for today?

Write out a verse from this chapter to **Memorize** this week:

> "And beginning with Moses and all the prophets, he interpreted to them in all the Scriptures the things concerning himself."
> ~ *Luke 24:27*

8

Acts 8:1-40

A Faith that is Alive

Many of you might be able to remember Rich Little, who made a living impersonating people. He could make you think that you were literally standing there with the person he was impersonating. Or, you might remember years back when everyone wanted to be like Michael Jordan, especially when everyone was singing, "Like Mike, if I could be like Mike!" Acts 8 focuses most of its time on the ministry of Philip, one of the disciples, who not only desired to be like Christ, but his faith was alive, like James, who later said, "Faith without works is dead."

The chapter opened with a word about Saul (who will be covered next time and beyond), but for the most part, this chapter centered on Philip. Rather than staying in the shade of the temple or huddling with the ones he knew, Philip launched out to not just any city, he went to Samaria. Jesus had told them to do this (Acts 1:8), but you have to understand that Samaria, historically, was the center of paganism in Israel (1 & 2 Kings).

When the kingdom after Solomon divided, Samaria became the capital of Israel and every single king "did evil in the sight of Lord." False worship, sexual immorality, child sacrifice, and murder were among the many evils done in Samaria. So, when the Holy Spirit began to scatter the persecuted believers, Philip didn't take the easy way out: he went to the hot spot of spiritual warfare!

When he arrived and began to preach the Gospel, he found plenty of people desperate to listen, hopeless and lost in generations of idolatry. He also found the lurking, prowling influence of Satan on every corner (1 Pet. 5:8). He ran into Simon, the magician who thought he could buy the favor of God. Simon was so self-centered that he could not see the real power of the Holy Spirit. Peter spoke the truth plainly to Simon (8:20-24), and who knows, God may have turned his heart around eventually. What we do know is that Philip had the heart to share Christ with anyone, anywhere.

The next story bears that out when Philip obediently went south and met the Ethiopian eunuch. What a great example of compassion and strategy as Philip was invited to ride with this man, opened the Scriptures to answer his questions, and then led him to faith in Christ. That's the kind of Gospel sharing that makes an impact. That's the kind of faith that is alive! He listened to the Spirit, obeyed, and then lovingly took him through the Bible to Jesus! Don't allow your faith to look dead and lifeless. If you want an exciting, Christ-honoring faith then listen, look, obey, and share! And then, you will begin to look more and more like Jesus. He's the one we really want to imitate!

President Calvin Coolidge invited some people from his hometown to dinner at the White House. Since they did not know how to behave at such an occasion, they thought the best policy would be just to do what the President did. The time came for serving coffee. The President poured his coffee into a saucer. As soon as the home folk saw it, they did the same. The next step for the President was to pour some milk and add a little sugar to the coffee in the saucer. The home folks did the same. They thought for sure that the next step would be for the President to take the saucer with the coffee and begin sipping it. But the President didn't do so. He leaned over, placed the saucer on the floor and called the cat.

Imitate Jesus! Watch Him carefully. He may be leaning over to feed the cat because He is their provider too. Or, the Lord may be showing you how to love others like He does. Either way, you can't go wrong!

Read Acts 8:1-40   Date: _____

GRASP
BIBLE JOURNAL PERSONAL NOTES

G   What **Grabbed** your attention, confused you or stood out?

R   What did you **Realize** about God and the people in this passage?

God?

People?

A How could you **Apply** this to your life?

> *Is there a sin to avoid?*
> *Is there a command to obey?*
> *Is there a promise to claim?*
> *Is there an example to follow?*
> *Is there a truth to know?*

S What is one **Specific** thing you could do this week to apply the truth from this passage? Write out "I will…".

P Write a **Prayer** of commitment to the Lord.

What are you **Thankful** for today?

Write out a verse from this chapter to **Memorize** this week:

"The gospel of peace is too good to keep to oneself."
~ Lailah Gifty Akita

9

Acts 9:1-43

New Life in Christ

Nicky Cruz was a notorious gang warlord in New York City for the Mau Maus. He was a bad dude! Fighting, maiming, stealing, and killing were his passions, until David Wilkerson, a country preacher from Pennsylvania heard a call through an article in Life Magazine about teens in NYC wreaking havoc on neighborhoods. David and his wife went to this neighborhood and met this gang.

As David and his wife displayed the love of Christ to this gang, Nicky, who never trusted anyone, decided to put together a rumble with a rival gang during a crusade held by David across the street. When Nicky heard the message of the Cross, he was broken. He gave his life to Christ and became a preacher of the Gospel. Nicky later started the ministry Teen Challenge. Their story is recorded in the book: *The Cross and the Switchblade.*

Transformation of a person's life is what Jesus does when the Gospel is realized. This happened to Saul, the infamous persecutor of the early Church. Saul (who we all now know as Paul), wanted to go to Damascus and bring to trial more Christians. His intent was to destroy this new movement. However, on the way, the Lord knocked him off his horse of pride and blinded him. Symbolically, this was a picture of every person who was lost. The god of this world had blinded their eyes (2 Cor. 4:4). As Jesus spoke to Saul, Paul's life and purpose were changed! Ananias was called on to disciple Saul and quickly, Saul went from a gang-banger against Christians to an evangelist and teacher! That's what Jesus can do! That's what new life is all about!

When Jesus changes you, He changes everything! That means you have a new identity, a new purpose, new direction, new passions, new loves and a new community. When the Church was afraid of Saul because of his past, Barnabas stepped in to assure them that Saul was a new man. Everyone needs a community of faith around them. You can be that community of faith for someone else who has struggled in life but now they know Christ and need community to surround them.

There are Nick Cruz's everywhere. Men and women, teens and children who are on their Damascus Road. They need healing like Peter gave and a person who will come to their rescue. Be the change that others need to experience as you live for Christ. Pray for a heart like David Wilkerson, Ananias, Barnabas and Peter. See people as Jesus sees them and tell them of the hope inside of you!

Read Acts 9:1-43   Date: _____

GRASP
BIBLE JOURNAL PERSONAL NOTES

G   What **Grabbed** your attention, confused you or stood out?

R   What did you **Realize** about God and the people in this passage?

God?

People?

A How could you **Apply** this to your life?

> *Is there a sin to avoid?*
> *Is there a command to obey?*
> *Is there a promise to claim?*
> *Is there an example to follow?*
> *Is there a truth to know?*

S What is one **Specific** thing you could do this week to apply the truth from this passage? Write out "I will…".

P Write a **Prayer** of commitment to the Lord.

What are you **Thankful** for today?

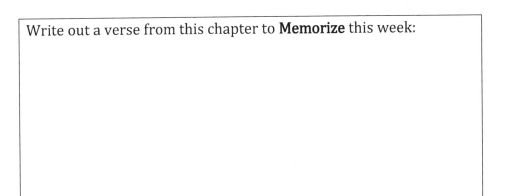

"All change comes from deepening your understanding of the salvation of Christ and living out the changes that understanding creates in your heart."
~ *Timothy Keller*

10

Acts 10:1-48

Our Mission is Everyone!

The story is told about a momma bird who knew it was time for her little ones to get out of the nest and fly on their own. One by one, they all stepped out, opened their wings, and flew, except the last one. He clung to the branches, resisting with all his might. The momma bird nudged him out on the limb, but the little bird only clung tighter. Finally, the momma bird used her beak to poke the talons of her little eaglet until he let go of the branch. Falling toward the forest floor, the little bird spread his wings, and just before hitting the ground, he soared to the heavens. Sometimes we need a push to get us moving!

The early Church had tested the waters a bit, going out of Jerusalem, but now the Lord wanted them to go further. More people needed to hear the Gospel and not just the Jews. Cornelius, a centurion of the Italian Cohort, a devout man who was generous and a seeker of God, lived in Caesarea (a place on the Mediterranean). He received a vision from the Lord about Peter.

As you read this wonderful story, it's great to see how God shows us the ways He has designed people to hear about Him. While the Lord has shown up so many times in people's dreams, especially in Muslim countries and unreached people groups, He always joins a believer with them so the believer can explain the gospel. Cornelius was a moral, God-seeking man, but he did not know Jesus! He needed to hear the gospel!

Peter received a vision about the gospel going to the Gentiles and ended up going to Caesarea to visit Cornelius. The story shows God's plan for people from all walks of life to hear the gospel from all manner of people.

This Gentile Pentecost (10:44-48) demonstrated three key principles that Tony Merida brings out in his work on Acts:

(1) We can show no hesitation in befriending people, unlike us (v. 20).

(2) We can show hospitality toward everyone, opening our homes and lives to them (v. 23).

(3) We can show humility before all people, regardless of their skin color or annual income, living with the understanding that we're all made in God's image (v. 26).

Elitism can find its way into the church when we hesitate or refuse to associate with people unlike us. That's what this chapter shows, that

God is the Creator of ALL people. Therefore, look around! You may just find your mission...you may just find your Cornelius!

Read Acts 10:1-48   Date: _____

GRASP
BIBLE JOURNAL PERSONAL NOTES

G   What **Grabbed** your attention, confused you or stood out?

R   What did you **Realize** about God and the people in this passage?

God?

People?

A   How could you **Apply** this to your life?

> *Is there a sin to avoid?*
> *Is there a command to obey?*
> *Is there a promise to claim?*
> *Is there an example to follow?*
> *Is there a truth to know?*

S   What is one **Specific** thing you could do this week to apply the truth from this passage? Write out "I will…".

P   Write a **Prayer** of commitment to the Lord.

What are you **Thankful** for today?

Write out a verse from this chapter to **Memorize** this week:

"We are called to take his light to a world where wrong seems right what could be too great a cost for sharing life with one who is lost?"
~ *Greg Nelson*

11

Acts 11:1-30

A Heart Like His

In 1271, Nicolo and Matteo Polo (father and uncle to Marco Polo) met with Kublai Khan, the known ruler of the East. As Khan heard the gospel, he was so intrigued that he requested the men bring 100 missionaries to share the message with his high officials and spread the gospel all across the East. However, the Pope replied, "Those barbarians do not deserve the gospel." For 30 years, nothing was done, and within a short period, Buddhists came in and converted the East to Buddhism. What a tragic failure to obey the clear command of God and take the gospel to the nations without prejudice!

Peter went up to Jerusalem and shared with certain leaders who still held to circumcision about his visit with the Gentile Centurion, Cornelius. He described the vision of crossing over into Gentile culture for the sake of the gospel. He described the same thing that happened to them at Pentecost in Acts 2. Peter explained his position well: "If then God gave the same gift to them as he gave to us when we believed in the Lord Jesus Christ, who was I that I could stand in God's way?"

That realization was critical for Peter's heart to be aligned with God's heart. How often do we look through our prejudices and rationalize how we do or do not respond to needs or to people? We see people through the lens of color, status, likeability, or some value we place on our time with them. Those distinctions are barriers to God's work. We are not called to make distinctions but to love without prejudice and to share the truth for the purpose of redemption, not condemnation.

Barnabas was sent to Antioch, where Gentiles were being saved, and "he was glad, and he exhorted them all to remain faithful to the Lord with steadfast purpose, for he was a good man, full of the Holy Spirit and of faith." Barnabas was the kind of Christian that modeled the heart of Christ. He rejoiced when he saw people unlike him come to Christ! He knew the gospel was for the world, and he wanted everyone to know Christ.

Antioch became the first place where the word Christian (Christ follower) was used. From that launching point, the gospel goes West, and the love of God for people they have never met dominates their ministry (2 Cor. 8). The best thing to do is not stand in God's way. He has a path and purpose. Get his heart, and follow it today!

William Booth, founder of the Salvation Army, at the end of a speech said, "While women weep, as they do now, I'll fight; while little children go hungry, I'll fight; while men go to prison, in and out, in and out, as they do now, I'll fight; while there is a drunkard left, while there is a poor lost girl in the streets, where there remains one dark soul without the light of God – I'll fight! I'll fight to the very end!"

Read Acts 11:1-30   Date: _____

GRASP
BIBLE JOURNAL PERSONAL NOTES

G   What **Grabbed** your attention, confused you or stood out?

R What did you **Realize** about God and the people in this passage?

God?

People?

A How could you **Apply** this to your life?

> *Is there a sin to avoid?*
> *Is there a command to obey?*
> *Is there a promise to claim?*
> *Is there an example to follow?*
> *Is there a truth to know?*

S What is one **Specific** thing you could do this week to apply the truth from this passage? Write out "I will…".

P Write a **Prayer** of commitment to the Lord.

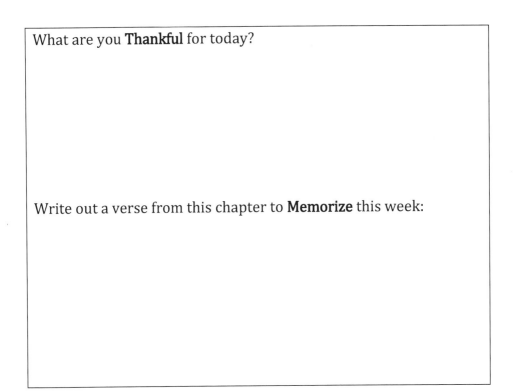

"The best and most beautiful things in the world cannot be seen or even touched – they must be felt with the heart."
~ Helen Keller

12

Acts 12:1-25

The Storm Before the Calm

John Stott wrote: "Indeed, throughout church history, the pendulum has swung between expansion and opposition, growth and shrinkage, advance and retreat, although with the assurance that even the powers of death and hell will never prevail against Christ's church since it is built securely on the rock."

As the Church was about to launch into its first missionary journey (Acts 13), Luke stopped to share with us some bad news and some good news ... a lesson in the high cost of following Jesus, a lesson in prayer, and a lesson in God having the final word. Herod had killed James, the brother of John with the sword. This was Herod Agrippa I, the only one of the Herods who killed ruthlessly (Herod the Great slaughtered the babies in Mt. 1:16-18; Herod Antipas beheaded John the Baptist, and Herod Agrippa II will appear later in Acts).

Herod went after James to see how the crowd would react before going for the big prize, Peter, the leader of the Church. Notice the contrast. When Herod picked up the sword, those of the church were on their knees in prayer. This is how Christians must respond during times of great trial!

In the midst of a major storm of murder, imprisonment, and persecution, there is calm. Peter, who has been arrested, is sleeping soundly between two Roman guards. Why not? The Church is praying, his life is in the hands of Jesus, and all Peter may be dreaming about is how many times he was with Jesus when Jesus calmed the storms around him! We go from storm to calm, valley to mountain top, and death to life. A follower of Jesus should never be anxious because we have His unshakeable peace (Phil. 4:6).

That assurance in Christ should make us unwaveringly confident when we pray. One of the most humorous moments in this chapter is when Peter is rescued and stands in front of Rhoda as she looks on in amazement. She has heard the prayers for deliverance offered up for Peter, but now he is standing there! When she runs to tell everyone, they don't believe it! How amazing it is when we pray, saying that we believe God can do everything, and then when God answers, we can't believe it!

Prayer is not just about asking God but believing God (Eph. 3:20). John Newton penned: "Thou art coming to a King, large petitions with thee bring for his grace and power are such; none can never ask too much." If you are facing a storm, stay calm, pray, and know God will take care of you! As God dealt with Herod (12:20-23), God will take care of each of His children! Trust Him 'n Pray!

Read Acts 12:1-25   Date: _____

GRASP
BIBLE JOURNAL PERSONAL NOTES

G   What **Grabbed** your attention, confused you or stood out?

R   What did you **Realize** about God and the people in this passage?

God?

People?

A   How could you **Apply** this to your life?

> *Is there a sin to avoid?*
> *Is there a command to obey?*
> *Is there a promise to claim?*
> *Is there an example to follow?*
> *Is there a truth to know?*

S   What is one **Specific** thing you could do this week to apply the truth from this passage? Write out "I will…".

P   Write a **Prayer** of commitment to the Lord.

What are you **Thankful** for today?

Write out a verse from this chapter to **Memorize** this week:

"Prayer is the key note of the most sanctified life, of the holiest ministry. He does the most for God who is the highest skilled in prayer."
~ *E.M. Bound*

13

Acts 13:1-52

Sent Out

A one-legged school teacher from Scotland came to J. Hudson Taylor to offer himself for service in China. "With only one leg, why do you think of going as a missionary?" Asked Taylor. "I do not see those with two legs going," replied George Scott. He was accepted.

It has been said, "We won't reach the nations apart from personal sacrifice." To this point in Acts, people have been pushed out of the comfortable nest of Jerusalem and into places like Antioch doing evangelism, mercy ministry, discipleship and church-supported mission's ministry. Now, two of their own are being sent out of the region, out of the country to nations filled with paganism and unfamiliar with the Good News of the gospel. While Acts 13 and 14 cover the first missionary journey of Saul and Barnabas and give us insight into international missions, "people who cross the street to bear witness to Jesus can also find much instruction and inspiration" (Merida).

Being sent should never come from a place of obvious talent or skill or personality, but of calling. The Holy Spirit called Saul and Barnabas. The Church responded after a season of fasting and prayer! That's the way you start a mission. So, Saul and Barnabas sailed to Cyprus and taught the Word of God in the synagogue. That was Saul's strategy. He was strategic in that he took the Word to the people who might be most familiar and then spread it outward.
When you think about being on mission, you have to keep in mind what you see here: (1) Some people will be open to God's Word (13:4- 7); (2) Some people will oppose God's Word (13:8-11) and (3) Some people will embrace God's Word (13:12) (Merida). Always remember that God is at work all around you. When people see a bold witness, who clearly articulates truth, they are drawn in by the Holy Spirit. Your job is to spread the seed.

You don't know who will receive it and who will reject it or who just needs more time to think on it. Saul and Barnabas cast the seed and let the Holy Spirit do His work, His way even in the presence of people who were not genuine.

From this spot, the team sailed to the mainland of modern Turkey and took on the physically grueling terrain, harsh conditions and abandonment of one of their helpers (3:13). Sometimes, the allure of travel on a mission trip grows old, and we long for the comforts of home. Paul and Barnabas persevered and Paul preached the gospel from a historical narrative that the Jews could understand. As the gospel took hold, persecution followed. Expect it! God's work will always be followed by God's opponents, but speak out boldly! Where are you being sent? To the nations or across the street to people living close to you. Missions are as close or far as you are willing to trust God and pray for people!

Read Acts 13:1-52   Date: _____

GRASP
BIBLE JOURNAL PERSONAL NOTES

G   What **Grabbed** your attention, confused you or stood out?

R   What did you **Realize** about God and the people in this passage?

God?

People?

A   How could you **Apply** this to your life?

> Is there a sin to avoid?
> Is there a command to obey?
> Is there a promise to claim?
> Is there an example to follow?
> Is there a truth to know?

S   What is one **Specific** thing you could do this week to apply the truth from this passage? Write out "I will...".

P   Write a **Prayer** of commitment to the Lord.

What are you **Thankful** for today?

Write out a verse from this chapter to **Memorize** this week:

"I'm not afraid of failure. I'm afraid of succeeding at things that don't matter."
~ *William Carey*

14

Acts 14:1-28

Living for the Glory of One

Leighton Ford, in his book, *Good News is for Sharing*, tells the story of an archaeologists digging in the remains of a school in Rome. They found a picture dating from the third century. It shows a boy standing, his hand raised, worshiping a figure on a cross, a figure that looks like a man with the head of an ass. Scrawled in the writing of a young person are the words, "Alexamenos worships his God." Nearby in a second inscription: "Alexamenos is faithful." Apparently, a young man who was a Christian was being mocked by his schoolmates for his faithful witness. But he was not ashamed; he was faithful.

Lewis Mumford wrote, "A certain amount of opposition is a great help to a man. Kites rise against, not with, the wind." Opposition is what Paul and Barnabas felt as they embarked on their first missionary journey. Jews and Greeks alike were believing the gospel and giving their life over to follow Jesus Christ. Unbelieving Jews, however, felt a tremendous threat to their faith and did as so many do: they poisoned the minds of people who would have believed. Here is the power of the gospel and the nature of the gospel. The power of the gospel changes minds, changes hearts, and moves people from their idolatrous, religious, selfish lives to a selfless loyalty to Christ that causes them to abandon all for the cause of Christ. The nature of the gospel drives a stake in the ground and says, "Here I stand!"

Paul would write to the Corinthians, "For the word of the cross is folly to those who are perishing, but to us who are being saved, it is the power of God." You will never be able to have harmony with everyone in the world because true harmony can only come through two parties in full agreement. Those opposed to the gospel may tolerate you and you them, but you will never be able to fully agree on what life is truly all about. Christians are called to love, care, speak the truth, and glorify God with every ounce of their life. The worst thing for the Church would be for it to compromise and take on the values of the world. That is happening enough!

Christians also are aware that their life is not their own, and that means every part of their lives. In this chapter, Paul and Barnabas are faced with a temptation that some cannot resist. When the crippled man is healed by Paul, the people (remember they have been worshipping idols all this time) want to make them gods. Paul and Barnabas react the right way by "rushing out into the crowd," pointing the people away from them to God! What a sermon on the spot!!

Again, as the team traveled, opposition followed. This time, Paul was stoned and almost died. However, like the other times, Paul gets right back in it with nothing deterring him from sharing the gospel. What is it about a sold-out follower of Jesus Christ who truly understands that a soul apart from the applied blood of Jesus cannot inherit eternal life but an eternity in hell makes them want to continue going into hostile territory without fear for their lives? It has to be their love for God and His glory! That's where love for people originates! When our love for God moves us to reckless abandonment, then our lives become contagiously attractive to others, and we live for the glory of the One!

Read Acts 14:1-28   Date: _____

GRASP
BIBLE JOURNAL PERSONAL NOTES

G   What **Grabbed** your attention, confused you or stood out?

R   What did you **Realize** about God and the people in this passage?

God?

People?

A   How could you **Apply** this to your life?

> *Is there a sin to avoid?*
> *Is there a command to obey?*
> *Is there a promise to claim?*
> *Is there an example to follow?*
> *Is there a truth to know?*

S What is one **Specific** thing you could do this week to apply the truth from this passage? Write out "I will…".

P Write a **Prayer** of commitment to the Lord.

What are you **Thankful** for today?

Write out a verse from this chapter to **Memorize** this week:

> "The glory of God, and, as our only means of glorifying him, the salvation of human souls, is the real business of life."
> ~ C.S. Lewis

15

Acts 15:1-41

Solo Fide!

R.C. Sproul wrote: "No Christian can avoid theology. Every Christian has a theology. The issue is not whether we want to have a theology. That's a given. The real issue is, do we have a sound theology? Do we embrace a true or false doctrine?" Now that the Gospel was going to the nations, Christianity and the message of salvation through Jesus Christ were spreading into places outside the Jewish traditions and practices.

For Jews, to be connected to God meant that you had to be circumcised. So, when Paul and Barnabas came back from their first missionary journey and reported how Gentiles were believing in Jesus, being filled with the Holy Spirit, and how their lives were changing, the Jewish believers in Jerusalem rejoiced. Still, some questioned whether a Gentile could truly be saved without taking the next step of circumcision.

Circumcision was a part of the Mosaic covenant but had become evidence of a person's faith in God. In reality, circumcision had become more important than anything. To the Jewish leaders, living a holy life for God was secondary to being circumcised. That was not the problem with Paul and Barnabas. They believed that holding a person to circumcision was the same as saying Jesus' death and resurrection were not enough to save a person and that another step had to be added for a person to truly be saved. At the Jerusalem Council, Paul could take the debate no longer.

He boldly stated that God gave the believing Gentiles the same Holy Spirit, making no distinction between Jew and Gentile, and cleansed their hearts by faith! The message was clear: salvation comes by grace through faith alone. James, the half-brother of Jesus and writer of the Book of James, stepped in. He compromised, not the Gospel, but for the sake of Jew-Gentile fellowship, with a ritual requirement from the Law. This moved the conversation away from circumcision to conduct, which Gentile believers could understand since they longed to live holy lives before God.

James's effort is a great commentary on how Christians should never compromise doctrine but be willing to find other ways to maintain fellowship. Fellowship will always be tested, especially when varying personalities, traditions, convictions, and past experiences are involved. This became quite clear when Paul and Barnabas sharply disagreed about bringing John Mark back on the road.

For a while, Paul and Barnabas were at odds, but somewhere down the line, peace and unity prevailed, as we will see. Don't ever let the enemy allow you to compromise the gospel or divide you relationally from your brothers or sisters in Christ! The gospel has to stand without being watered down and always announce that salvation is by grace through faith alone! With it, find ways to build bridges so a conversation can continue.

Read Acts 15:1-41   Date: _____

GRASP
BIBLE JOURNAL PERSONAL NOTES

G   What **Grabbed** your attention, confused you or stood out?

R   What did you **Realize** about God and the people in this passage?

   God?

   People?

A   How could you **Apply** this to your life?

> *Is there a sin to avoid?*
> *Is there a command to obey?*
> *Is there a promise to claim?*
> *Is there an example to follow?*
> *Is there a truth to know?*

S   What is one **Specific** thing you could do this week to apply the truth from this passage? Write out "I will…".

P   Write a **Prayer** of commitment to the Lord.

What are you **Thankful** for today?

Write out a verse from this chapter to **Memorize** this week:

"It is faith – without good works and prior to good works – that takes us to heaven. We come to God through faith alone."
~ Martin Luther

16

Acts 16:1-40

The Miracle at Midnight

This chapter is a favorite in Acts for many people. It may also be one of the most popular chapters and stories in the Bible. The chapter opens with Paul and Silas picking up a new ministry companion, a young man named Timothy (yes, 1 & 2 Timothy is named after him). They are hindered by the Spirit from ministry in Galatia, so the Lord gives Paul a vision of a Macedonian man calling for help. In response, they set sail for the eastern coast of Greece, making their way through some towns before settling in Philippi.

Philippi dates back to 360 BCE and became the prima regio (prime region, first in importance) for Romans after their conquest in 168 BCE. With the construction of the via Egnatia, a road to the Adriatic Sea, Philippi became a major trade city. One of those traders was a woman from Thyatira named Lydia. She believed in God but had not heard the gospel of Jesus. When Paul shared the gospel, she believed and became the first baptized convert in Europe! Through Lydia's partnership, God brought the gospel to be much of Europe. God uses all sorts of people to expand His kingdom.

Here is a successful woman who used her means to support the gospel's work wherever it could be shared! Rather than hoarding her money, she invested it in people knowing Christ! While in Philippi, Paul cast out a demon from a little girl who was being prostituted for her fortune-telling.

Her owners were ticked off and took them before the magistrates, who beat them and put them under house arrest. At midnight, as they sang and praised the Lord loudly, the Lord shook off their chains, but they stayed in prison, knowing that if they left, the jailor and probably his family would be punished or killed. What a heart for people! When Paul and the others could have escaped, even after being beaten, they cared more for the souls of their enemy than their own lives.

What do you care about more than your own life? Most of us might say our spouse or our children, but what about a stranger? In our current culture, we are more polarized and fragmented than ever before. Who has time for a stranger? Identity politics, racial divisions, and religious tribalism have kept people at arms lengths. If a person doesn't agree with us, then we have no room in our lives for them. Paul was not this way. He worshiped Christ openly and allowed the Holy Spirit to move in people's hearts. They were beaten, stoned, ridiculed, and rejected, but still, they preached Jesus.

No wonder we still have this story 2,000 years later. What do you care about more than anything else? Your family? Your career? Your house? Your 401k? What if everything was gone? What would you care about then? The miracle at midnight was not that the men were delivered. That had already happened in Christ. The miracle was that they stayed, loved, and shared Jesus!

Read Acts 16:1-40   Date: _____

GRASP
BIBLE JOURNAL PERSONAL NOTES

G   What **Grabbed** your attention, confused you or stood out?

R   What did you **Realize** about God and the people in this passage?

God?

People?

A How could you **Apply** this to your life?

> *Is there a sin to avoid?*
> *Is there a command to obey?*
> *Is there a promise to claim?*
> *Is there an example to follow?*
> *Is there a truth to know?*

S What is one **Specific** thing you could do this week to apply the truth from this passage? Write out "I will...".

P Write a **Prayer** of commitment to the Lord.

What are you **Thankful** for today?

Write out a verse from this chapter to **Memorize** this week:

> "God has given believers the responsibility to share the gospel to all the world, and we need to use all at our disposal to accomplish this task."
> ~ *Theodore Epp*

17

Acts 17:1-34

Turning the World Upside Down

As Paul and Silas made their way from Philippi, they moved south, eventually coming to Thessalonica. Like before, Paul entered the synagogue and preached the gospel. Once again, they were persecuted and accused of turning the world upside down! That's what you call "Making an impact!" Dr. John Geddie, a Presbyterian missionary, went to Aneityum, an island in the South Pacific, in 1848 and worked there for God for 24 years. On a tablet erected to his memory in the church where he preached, these words are inscribed: When he landed in 1848, there were no Christians. When he left in 1872, there were no heathens.

Every Christian can make an impact. It's when they see a need and respond with the love and truth of Christ that things begin to change. When Paul was escorted out of Thessalonica, he was taken to Athens. When he arrived, "his spirit was provoked within him as he saw that the city was full of idols." Our world and our lives are surrounded by idols. They loom large in our lives in the form of possessions we envy, positions we desire, and people we worship. In his book *Counterfeit Gods*, Tim Keller writes: "The true god of your heart is what your thoughts effortlessly go to when there is nothing else demanding your attention." What do your thoughts effortlessly go to?

For the people in Athens, their city was full of idols, and for Paul, who knew that Jesus Christ had come to die for the souls of people who aimlessly followed man's imaginations of deities and leaders who led ignorant people down that path, he was angry! As he approached the Areopagus, he preached the gospel to the intellectual elite and called them to repentance. Paul revealed to them the "unknown god," whom they worshiped without knowing who he might be.

The Athenians were trying to cover all their bases. So many people do this by going to church, some living the Golden Rule, serving a charity, and trying to live their best life. Moral reformation, while it seems good, falls short of the standard for salvation because it bypasses the sacrifice of Jesus. Paul spoke plainly to the people that God who created them does not dwell in human-built temples and made from one man all the nations "that they should seek God, and perhaps feel their way toward him and find him."

While they worshiped idols of silver and gold made from man's imagination, God was not like that because he came to us as a man, died in our place, and conquered death through his resurrection. When we preach the gospel and live the gospel, we become world changers. You cannot save someone, but you can introduce them to Someone who can! Turn your community upside down for Christ. Where will you start?

Read Acts 17:1-34   Date: _____

GRASP
BIBLE JOURNAL PERSONAL NOTES

G   What **Grabbed** your attention, confused you or stood out?

R   What did you **Realize** about God and the people in this passage?

God?

People?

A How could you **Apply** this to your life?

> *Is there a sin to avoid?*
> *Is there a command to obey?*
> *Is there a promise to claim?*
> *Is there an example to follow?*
> *Is there a truth to know?*

S What is one **Specific** thing you could do this week to apply the truth from this passage? Write out "I will…".

P Write a **Prayer** of commitment to the Lord.

What are you **Thankful** for today?

Write out a verse from this chapter to **Memorize** this week:

"Every single person has the power to change the world and help people."
~ *Laura Marano*

18

Acts 18:1-28

Press On Under the Pressures

There is a cartoon of a man in his 80s chuckling as he hears a young pastor say, "Who said the ministry is stressful? I'm 35 and feel great!" No one who has been in ministry very long or has invested their lives in people for very long understands better how draining ministry can be. You go to meetings where the Sunday before, a man is sweet, singing about Jesus, and serves at the door as a greeter, but in that meeting, you think he is the spawn of Satan! Or, you are friends with a person one moment, and the next, they put the proverbial knife in your back ... publicly. Ministry is no joke!

Paul understood this all too well. As Paul left Athens, he continued south to Corinth. Corinth was a port city with people from all over the world. He met two people, Aquila and Priscilla, who were tentmakers, and they worked together. Paul continued his strategy of preaching first in the synagogues and, as usual, faced intense opposition. This time Paul had had enough!! He stormed out, basically saying, "If you want to face God on your own, then do it! I'm fed up with you. I'm out!"

Sometimes ministry can tire us, and people can get us so frustrated that we don't see the point or have the energy to keep going. Don't you just love the patience and compassion of our Lord? When Paul is frustrated, and about to lose his cool in a bad way, the Lord comes to him like he did Elijah in 1 Kings 19 and encourages him. Words of encouragement can keep a person invested longer when everything in him wants to throw in the towel. Paul stayed, and God birthed a new church. Even as the persecution continued, he kept on preaching.

Finally, he left with his new ministry partners and made his way back to Antioch. Before he arrived back home, he stopped in Ephesus. He promised them that he would be back if God willed. That promise would be fulfilled, and a mighty church would be planted. Not only that, but they were able to disciple a young man named Apollos to a fuller understanding of the Gospel, and he went on to make a major impact among the Jews, seeing many of them come to faith in Christ.

You see, sometimes in ministry, you need to step away and get some rest. In those moments, God speaks tenderly in our ears of His grace, love, and care for us. He encourages us with his word and puts people in our lives who speak kindly so that we can receive it. When this happens, we are rejuvenated, energized, and refueled for another rigorous season of ministry. Yes, ministry to people can be draining and filled with unappreciation, but know that the Lord is with you wherever you go. He will walk you through the hardships and strengthen you in the rough places. Find a place of rest. Talk to your Father. Lean on the everlasting arms of Jesus.

Read Acts 18:1-28   Date: _____

GRASP
BIBLE JOURNAL PERSONAL NOTES

G   What **Grabbed** your attention, confused you or stood out?

R   What did you **Realize** about God and the people in this passage?

God?

People?

A How could you **Apply** this to your life?

> *Is there a sin to avoid?*
> *Is there a command to obey?*
> *Is there a promise to claim?*
> *Is there an example to follow?*
> *Is there a truth to know?*

S What is one **Specific** thing you could do this week to apply the truth from this passage? Write out "I will…".

P Write a **Prayer** of commitment to the Lord.

What are you **Thankful** for today?

Write out a verse from this chapter to **Memorize** this week:

"When I cannot read, when I cannot think, when I cannot even pray, I can trust."
~ *Hudson Taylor*

19

Acts 19:1-41

From Darkness to His Glorious Light

Some years ago, a young man walked into a pastor's office, visibly shaking. For the next hour, he explained how we had given his life over to Satan through witchcraft. He described the practices, the instruments used, and the spells he would cast. The darkness of that conversation was noticeable until the pastor began to explain the

Gospel of Jesus Christ. Just as quickly as the darkness flooded that office, the light of Christ dispersed the darkness, and that young man was on his knees, forsaking Satan and himself for the grace, love, and forgiveness of Jesus! He walked out to his car and gave the pastor a box of witchcraft books, candles, and knives (which he burned). A few weeks later, that changed young man was baptized and began to serve in that church.

Paul was now on his third missionary journey and entered the major city of Ephesus. He would meet with everything from religious pretenders to people steeped in witchcraft to rioters of paganism. As he entered the city, Paul found "twelve almost Christians" who were religious but not followers of Christ. To their confession that they did not know there even was a Holy Spirit, Paul explained it further, and a mini-Pentecost broke out. At that moment in Acts, God did much like Acts 2, but this was not and is not the norm.

For most of Acts, the visual and verbal manifestation of the Spirit through tongues did not accompany salvation. Mostly, it was repentance, faith in Christ, and then baptism. For these new believers, God used various gifts in that moment to solidify their faith in extraordinary ways, probably due to the extreme pagan culture that surrounded them in Ephesus. After this, Paul confronted the seven sons of Sceva, and as a result, the name of Jesus proved no match for Satan.

People saw the power of Christ and immediately confessed their sins and brought their boxes of witchcraft to be burned. The power of the gospel impacted people's lives to the extreme, and they knew their conduct had to change. This is the power of Christ! Not every person has this radical change immediately, but the gospel works in a person to make them live, look and love more like Jesus.

Now, the next part (19:21-41) should give you chills! Paul confronted the corporate industries of pagan manufacturing and the pagan temple industry. This is where the money flowed, and the leaders were eager to call Paul out as someone who could ruin their lives. They had to hold Paul back from going straight into the crowd. There is always a time and a place for everything.

As God used this clerk to quiet the crowd, the lesson for us becomes clear: the kingdom of Christ is not grown through violence or extremism but through the simple message of the gospel. Christianity does not have to display its physical might but only display the grace and truth of Jesus!

Read Acts 19:1-41   Date: _____

GRASP
BIBLE JOURNAL PERSONAL NOTES

G   What **Grabbed** your attention, confused you or stood out?

R What did you **Realize** about God and the people in this passage?

God?

People?

A How could you **Apply** this to your life?

> Is there a sin to avoid?
> Is there a command to obey?
> Is there a promise to claim?
> Is there an example to follow?
> Is there a truth to know?

S What is one **Specific** thing you could do this week to apply the truth from this passage? Write out "I will…".

P Write a **Prayer** of commitment to the Lord.

What are you **Thankful** for today?

Write out a verse from this chapter to **Memorize** this week:

"The glory of the gospel is that when the church is absolutely different from the world, she invariably attracts it."
~ *Martyn Lloyd Jones*

20

Acts 20:1-38

Never Stop Being an Encourager

When you read chapter 20, the most famous part of the chapter is the humorous story, which could have been tragic, of Eutychus, a young man who fell asleep during Paul's sermon. Every preacher, teacher, or lecturer knows what it's like to look out over a congregation and see several people nodding off. The flesh is weak, especially during a long sermon at midnight. One evening during a college class, one of the students kept falling asleep and started snoring during the professor's lecture. The professor took an eraser and threw it at him. I don't think the student ever did that again!

While that story gets a lot of attention, the main point of Acts 20 is the importance of encouraging people in life and in ministry. No one knows how difficult life can be until they go through times of struggle. The chapter opens with encouragement and closes with encouragement. Paul knew that if the believers in all these places throughout Macedonia and Asia Minor (Turkey) would be able to minister effectively in the midst of persecution and hardships, he had to keep them encouraged. Listen, life is hard enough. When you add in ministry to people who have deep needs or people who actively reject your message, life can get almost hard to bear.

Encouragement is essential. Words of affirmation, a note, a text, an email, a phone call, or a card can be the difference between giving up and running hard to the finish line. Hebrews 3:12-13 says, "Watch out brothers and sisters so that there won't be in any of you an evil, unbelieving heart that turns away from the living God. But encourage each other daily, while it is still called today so that none of you is hardened by sin's deception." As George Adams wrote, "Encouragement is the oxygen of the soul." Pastor and writer Tony Merida wrote in his work on Acts, "We must encourage one another constantly. Our hearts are fickle; sin never sleeps; Satan is at work; and the gospel is of first importance." We all know how a word of encouragement can help when we are running or working out, or after we have attempted something and failed.

As Paul and his companions traveled through the region, he called for the elders, the church leaders, to meet him. His speech to them was instructive and encouraging. Paul exemplified a servant leader who pastored the flock of Christ well. This was how Paul built the churches. This is how Paul selected and taught the churches to select leaders. The Miletus address was moving, even to the point of tears, as Paul left them. Pastors are not CEOs or renegades or rock-stars.

Pastors that please the Lord encourage and teach their flock. By the way, you don't have to be a pastor to be a major encourager in another person's life. William Barclay once wrote: "One of the highest duties is the duty of encouragement...It is easy to laugh at men's ideals; it is easy to pour cold water on their enthusiasm; it is easy to discourage others. The world is full of discouragers. We have a Christian duty to encourage one another. Many a time a word of praise or thanks or appreciation or cheer has kept a man on his feet. Blessed is the man who speaks such a word."

Read Acts 20:1-38   Date: _____

GRASP
BIBLE JOURNAL PERSONAL NOTES

G   What **Grabbed** your attention, confused you or stood out?

R   What did you **Realize** about God and the people in this passage?

God?

People?

A   How could you **Apply** this to your life?

> *Is there a sin to avoid?*
> *Is there a command to obey?*
> *Is there a promise to claim?*
> *Is there an example to follow?*
> *Is there a truth to know?*

S   What is one **Specific** thing you could do this week to apply the truth from this passage? Write out "I will…".

P   Write a **Prayer** of commitment to the Lord.

What are you **Thankful** for today?

Write out a verse from this chapter to **Memorize** this week:

"Our chief want is someone who will inspire us to be what we know we could be."
~ Ralph Waldo Emerson

21

Acts 21:1-26

The Importance of Friendship

Tim Keller wrote in an article entitled, *Spiritual Friendship*, "To need and to want deep spiritual friendships is not a sign of spiritual immaturity but of maturity. It's not a sign of weakness, but a sign of health." From Acts 20:36 to Acts 21:1-16, we see the benefits and blessings of spiritual friendships, friendships with people who walk the same road you walk with Christ. That road is not always easy, and often, it's filled with heartache, trouble, rejection, misunderstandings, and discouragement. No one should walk with Christ alone.

We need friendships and community. Someone said, "When you become a Christian, you not only enter into a new relationship with God through Jesus, but you also enter into new relationships with other believers" (1 John 3:11-15). Don't wait until you need friends; cultivate them now so that when the need arises, they are right there.

Paul's friends were the ones urging him not to go to Jerusalem, trying to look out for his safety. However, they went with Paul and finally made it to James and the church leaders in Jerusalem. A missionary celebration erupted! Don't you love it when people get together sharing stories of God's goodness and His power to change lives? These stories encourage our hearts and compel us to greater faithfulness in the Gospel. We need to hear more of them!

James was concerned for Paul's safety because the Jews had twisted Paul's words to say that he did not believe a person should be circumcised or obey the law. Paul was clear that circumcision was not a requirement for salvation but never demanded that circumcision be eliminated. He continued to observe cultural traditions and through the power of the Holy Spirit, obeyed the Mosaic Law given through the Ten Commandments. Jesus had sais the same thing, that his purpose was not to destroy the law but to fulfill the law. Only through Christ and in the power of the Spirit can you fully obey the law.

Paul never compromised the Gospel or participated in sin. For the sake of spreading the teaching of the gospels, he went along with their traditions, just like you do when visiting Israel at the Wailing Wall or a Middle Eastern country with a strictly modest dress code. It would be the same worshipping with other believers in different cultures, such as in Africa or the jungles of Brazil.

Christians must be flexible without compromising the Gospel. It's healthy to get outside your subculture and see how God works among other people, how God is revealing himself to unbelievers throughout the world. In fact, it's incredible!! Merida writes, "We too should be flexible when ministering to various cultures. Some cultures are more traditional, while others are more progressive. When outside your immediate sphere, you may find it necessary to learn to adapt to the ways of another group for the sake of the Gospel's spread." Be friends with everyone you can and looks for ways to understand them.

Read Acts 21:1-26   Date: _____

GRASP
BIBLE JOURNAL PERSONAL NOTES

G   What **Grabbed** your attention, confused you or stood out?

R   What did you **Realize** about God and the people in this passage?

   God?

   People?

> *Is there a sin to avoid?*
> *Is there a command to obey?*
> *Is there a promise to claim?*
> *Is there an example to follow?*
> *Is there a truth to know?*

A   How could you **Apply** this to your life?

S   What is one **Specific** thing you could do this week to apply the truth from this passage? Write out "I will…".

P   Write a **Prayer** of commitment to the Lord.

What are you **Thankful** for today?

Write out a verse from this chapter to **Memorize** this week:

"I went out to find a friend and found none. I went out to be a friend and found many."
~ *Chinese Proverb*

22

Acts 21:27-22:29

Every Christian Has a Testimony

On the cover of a book by Max Lucado, the subtitle reads: "It's Amazing the Lengths God Will Go to Get Our Attention." The same can be said of what God did in the Apostle Paul's life. His story could be repeated by many people whom God delivered from a life bound for hell but rescued for eternity in Heaven. Paul's life and every other person whom Christ redeemed is a witness to the power of the gospel.

After Paul spent several days teaching in the Temple, he was arrested and beaten by a group of Jewish leaders who were out for blood. The Romans stepped in and arrested Paul, mainly to get to the bottom of the crisis. Paul asked permission to share his side of the story, and his request was granted. From that moment, Paul laid out his testimony in the most eloquent way. Every Christian has a testimony, a story about how they came to Christ.

For most people, their story would probably not make an article in Christianity Today, nor would Billy Graham ask them to share it at a crusade. However, no matter how a person came to Christ, their story is as valuable as those who have their testimony in print or online. Paul's defense is a great example of how to craft a faith story that can be shared with anyone. Everyone's story is different and can be shared at various points, but this story is really helpful for Christians to know how to share their own.

Paul first shared about his life before Christ (22:3-5). Everyone has a past, no matter how young they were when they accepted Christ. Even if your past is not all that "sinful", you can think about what was missing in your life before you came to believe in Jesus Christ. After Paul shared his past, he shared his encounter with Christ (22:6-11). We would all like to have a Damascus Road experience where we are knocked off a horse and blinded until someone baptizes us and we see the light once again! That would make for a great story to tell at a conference or write about ina book.

But for most people, theirs is a gradual understanding of the gospel or sometimes an abrupt understanding that brings a person face-to-face with Jesus. Sometimes, you don't even have to get that specific. You might just say, "I had a life-changing experience." Whet their appetite to want to know what happened to bring you from your lostness to deep peace, and then tell them how that peace has transformed your life.

The last section of Paul's faith story was about his commission to preach the gospel. That is everyone's commission in some way. We have been called out of darkness to God's glorious light to be His people and to live for His glory (1 Pet. 2:9-12).

There are times when your testimony will not be accepted, as Paul's was not. Never let that deter you. You may not get to continue but continue to love, share truth and pray. We live in a world that needs the light of Christ. Share your story where you can, and share the gospel everywhere you can!

Read Acts 21:27 – 22:29   Date: _____

GRASP
BIBLE JOURNAL PERSONAL NOTES

G   What **Grabbed** your attention, confused you or stood out?

R   What did you **Realize** about God and the people in this passage?

   God?

   People?

A How could you **Apply** this to your life?

> *Is there a sin to avoid?*
> *Is there a command to obey?*
> *Is there a promise to claim?*
> *Is there an example to follow?*
> *Is there a truth to know?*

S What is one **Specific** thing you could do this week to apply the truth from this passage? Write out "I will…".

P Write a **Prayer** of commitment to the Lord.

What are you **Thankful** for today?

Write out a verse from this chapter to **Memorize** this week:

"For I am not ashamed of the Gospel, for it is the power of God for salvation to everyone who believes, to the Jew first and also for the Greek."
~ *Romans 1:16*

23

Acts 22:30-23:35

Never Give Up!

When you hear someone say, "I'm really up against it," you instantly know they are experiencing a problem or crisis. The Apostle Paul could have said it many times in his life while he served Christ and shared the gospel. His life had been threatened over and over again. He had been stoned, beaten, and publicly maligned. This time, however, there was a conspiracy against him and a mob organized. The one thing they had on their mind was to kill him. Prior to this, Paul had been asked to explain his ministry actions to the Sanhedrin. While he was doing so, the High Priest slapped Paul! That was totally uncalled for and unbiblical. Paul responded with a rebuke.

He was right to do so, but Paul, who didn't know that the one who slapped him was the High Priest, showed respect for the office by issuing an apology seemingly to the group. When we face a moment of injustice, especially against us, like a slap to the face, it takes a tremendous amount of self-control to stop ourselves from reacting.

Paul said to the Corinthians, "When we are reviled, we bless them; when we are persecuted, we endure it" (1 Cor. 4:12). Jesus said something similar in Matthew 5:39. We need to call out hypocrisy, but we also need to operate our lives with restraint. The character displayed in Christ is more important than our pride.

The Jewish leaders devised the plot to kill Paul, and like a group of people wanting vigilante justice or a mob demanding the sheriff hand over his prisoner to them, they devised a plan for Paul to be handed over. Once the plan was discovered, they brought it to the head of the tribunal. The tribunal organized a garrison of soldiers with a letter and escorted Paul out of the city to Caesarea and a meeting with Felix, the governor.

As you read this chapter, you may be wondering what it is about this story that is so important. The answer is found in 23:11, "The following night the Lord stood by him and said, 'Take courage, for as you have testified to the facts about me in Jerusalem, so you must do in Rome." When Christ came to Paul, the Lord gave Paul the assurance he needed to press on! Who knows what Paul was going through during these days, but you can only imagine that he was going through some tough times.

Everywhere Paul went and preached the Gospel, he had people who accepted it enthusiastically and others who rejected it violently. Yet, Paul was ready in and out of season (2 Tim. 4:2). What kept him encouraged and moving ahead? The Lord reminded him of three things that we all need to know when discouraged (23:11):

(1) **Our strength is in His presence.** Jesus knew where Paul was and what he needed at that moment! "Take courage!" That's the Lord strengthening Paul!
(2) **Our affirmation, if obedient to Christ, is made clear by Christ.** Jesus encouraged Paul that He recognized his faithfulness.

(3) **Our purpose is not finished.** The Lord will still use you until your last breath!

Jim Valvano, former basketball coach for North Carolina State, famously gave speech while battling cancer, where he said, "Never give up! Don't ever give up!" Take that to heart today!

Read Acts 22:20 – 23:35   Date: _____

GRASP
BIBLE JOURNAL PERSONAL NOTES

G   What **Grabbed** your attention, confused you or stood out?

R   What did you **Realize** about God and the people in this passage?

God?

People?

A How could you **Apply** this to your life?

> *Is there a sin to avoid?*
> *Is there a command to obey?*
> *Is there a promise to claim?*
> *Is there an example to follow?*
> *Is there a truth to know?*

S What is one **Specific** thing you could do this week to apply the truth from this passage? Write out "I will...".

P Write a **Prayer** of commitment to the Lord.

What are you **Thankful** for today?

> Write out a verse from this chapter to **Memorize** this week:

"The Lord is my strength and my song."
~ Psalm 118:14

24

Acts 24:1-27

On Trial for the Gospel

When you hear the words, *Perry Mason* or *Matlock* or *A Few Good Men*, you think about a courtroom and the drama that ensues. Maybe you grew up watching *People's Court*, or more recently, you've seen *Judge Steve Harvey*. When you read Acts 24, it's like you have stepped into a courtroom, listening to the charges being brought, hearing the prosecution's opening statement, and then hearing the defense of the accused. This is what you get in the chapter as the High Priest, Ananias, brings down his hot-shot prosecutor, Tertullus, to lay out the charges against Paul. After flattering Governor Felix with sugar sticks and honey dripping from his lips, Tertullus turned to make his accusations.

He accused Paul of being a "plague," or you might say, a "pest" that infected the people (17:6-7). Tertullus then charged him with insurrection through rioting (which happened most of the time after Paul spoke), and called him the ringleader of the sect of the Nazarenes (possibly what Jewish Christians were called since it had a derogatory meaning). He finally charged Paul with profaning the temple.

What does all of this mean for us today? As Paul was pressed against and attacked for his faith, those who walk with Christ will experience the same on some level. "Do not be surprised at the fiery trial when it comes upon you to test you as though something strange was happening to you" (1 Pet. 4:12). So many in our culture thrive on living opposite of the values we see in Christ, and when we do not join them and adopt cultural values, they are surprised and malign us (4:3-4). Christians have to be prepared to fight a spiritual battle against evil, an evil that is tricky, allusive, and destructive (Eph. 6:1-10). When Paul's accuser was finished, Paul stepped up to give his defense.

His words were logical, articulate, and based on Scripture. Paul tied Christianity back to the Old Testament and the Law. Then, he laid out his case brilliantly and calmly, refuting clearly the charges one by one. Finally, Paul brought up the core of Christianity, without which our faith was worthless, which was the resurrection (24:21). He never had a conversation or preaching engagement where this was not brought to the forefront. That is so helpful for us as we converse with people. Our faith is meaningless and powerless if Christ is not raised (1 Cor. 15:17-21). Never leave that out.

Felix dismissed everyone but later called Paul to explain more about Jesus to him. As Felix and his wife listened, Paul spoke about righteousness, self-control, and the coming judgment. He was not just giving Felix an outline of Christian living, he was confronting him with man's depravity, God's holiness, and showing him his need for Jesus! Paul's example should be taken to heart. The content of the Gospel is God's holiness, man's sinfulness, and man's greatest need met through Jesus Christ.

Read Acts 24:1-27   Date: _____

GRASP
BIBLE JOURNAL PERSONAL NOTES

G   What **Grabbed** your attention, confused you or stood out?

R   What did you **Realize** about God and the people in this passage?

God?

People?

A   How could you **Apply** this to your life?

> *Is there a sin to avoid?*
> *Is there a command to obey?*
> *Is there a promise to claim?*
> *Is there an example to follow?*
> *Is there a truth to know?*

S   What is one **Specific** thing you could do this week to apply the truth from this passage? Write out "I will…".

P   Write a **Prayer** of commitment to the Lord.

What are you **Thankful** for today?

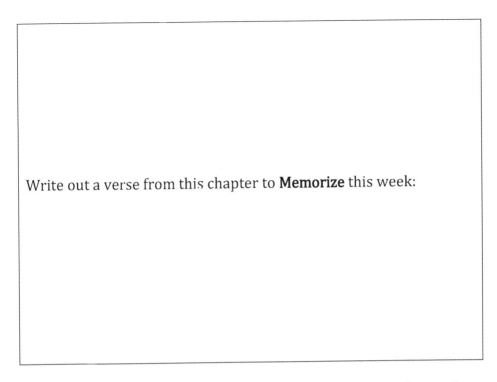

Write out a verse from this chapter to **Memorize** this week:

"Stand up, stand up for Jesus, ye soldiers of the cross. Lift high his royal banner, it must not suffer a loss."
~ *Bart Millard*

25

Acts 25:1-27

Trusting the Purpose and Plan of God

God is never delayed or undecided when fulfilling His promises. What He says, He will do, and at this moment in Paul's life, the Lord is about to show Paul that He can always be trusted. In Acts 23:11, the Lord appeared to Paul and said, "Take courage, for as you have testified to the facts about me in Jerusalem, so you must also testify in Rome." God's purpose for Paul was to expand the Gospel's reach and use Paul as the mouthpiece of the Gospel to the central city of the Roman Empire.

From Rome, the Gospel would spread throughout the world. As new leadership took place in Caesarea, Felix, who Emperor Nero fired, was replaced by Festus. Festus wasted no time getting to know his Jewish subjects and went to Jerusalem. He discovered that the Jews still wanted to kill a prisoner left over by Felix, Paul of Tarsus. Festus spoke to Paul on his return and found nothing of merit to charge him, but as a typical politician, he tried to play both sides of the fence. Festus asked Paul about going to Jerusalem to face charges, but Paul knew this was too dangerous. Finally, he took the only out he had left, and he appealed to Caesar. Festus agreed.

What you have to see in this passage is the sovereign hand of God working out His purposes in His time. Listen, God never does anything haphazardly. Everything God does has purpose, design, and forethought. There is nothing that God allows that will not, in the end, bring glory to His name, even when the event is horrific and confusing. We live in a world of sin that is not perfect. Man-made that choice, but God knew that by working through man's free will, He would be accused of not loving, not caring, or not caring enough to intervene. However, God has given us all we need for righteousness, but we have thrown it away for our self-rule. And look where that has left us.

As a society, we are more broken, more impoverished, more isolated, more immoral, more heartless, and more evil than ever. And yet, He is patient with us. He has given us life and peace through Jesus Christ. In the next chapter, Paul makes that known as he relates his story to another king, King Agrippa II. Agrippa was the great-grandson of Herod the Great and the son of Herod Agrippa I, who killed James and arrested Peter. He died under God's judgment (Acts

12). Agrippa and his sister arrived in Caesarea to visit Festus and, after hearing about his case, wanted to hear it from Paul. Paul shared the beautiful story of conversion and the power of the Gospel in Acts 26.

Throughout this story, you can see the hand of God. The Lord is working to put the pieces of the puzzle together so more people can hear the Good News of Christ. God is always at work around you and in you to fulfill His purpose. Trust Him with every moment, and watch Him do mighty things in you and through you!

Read Acts 25:1-27   Date: _____

GRASP
BIBLE JOURNAL PERSONAL NOTES

G   What **Grabbed** your attention, confused you or stood out?

R   What did you **Realize** about God and the people in this passage?

God?

People?

A   How could you **Apply** this to your life?

> Is there a sin to avoid?
> Is there a command to obey?
> Is there a promise to claim?
> Is there an example to follow?
> Is there a truth to know?

S   What is one **Specific** thing you could do this week to apply the truth from this passage? Write out "I will…".

P   Write a **Prayer** of commitment to the Lord.

What are you **Thankful** for today?

Write out a verse from this chapter to **Memorize** this week:

"When you were down to nothing, God is up to something. Stay strong. Pray and keep the faith."
~ *Germany Kent*

26

Acts 26:1-32

Here I Stand!

No one knows how difficult it is to face your accusers until you stand face-to-face with them. Christians have done this throughout the centuries with the threat of death all around them. In other countries, Christians are constantly threatened, beaten, and sometimes killed. To make a stand for Christ takes courage, determination, and trusting the promise of the Lord to be with them when their accuser stands to refute their faith in Jesus Christ as Lord (John 16:1-4). King Agrippa called on Paul to speak. Just as Paul had done on previous occasions, he stepped up to the moment and clearly articulated three of the most important truths about his story:

1. He was a sinner filled with religion and in need of God's promise.

2. Jesus was the fulfillment of that promise through his death and resurrection.

3. Every part of Jesus's story was tied back to the promises of the Old Testament.

Paul was clear that Jesus was the promised Messiah and his death and resurrection were proof.

This story is a wonderful example of articulating the gospel with clarity, logic, historical perspective, and details of the gospel that cannot be compromised. Listen to the boldness and conviction in Paul's words: "And now I stand here on trial because of my hope in the promise made by God to our fathers, to which our twelve tribes hope to attain, as they earnestly worship night and day…Why is it thought incredible by any of you that God raises the dead (26:6-8)?" This is where Paul would make his stand!

Martin Luther, the father of the Protestant Reformation, was a monk, priest, and professor in the Roman Catholic Church. As he read scripture, he came to terms with the fact that the corruption in the

Catholic church and the inconsistencies with scripture could not go on without opposition. Others had tried but had not been able to shut him down.

Finally, on October 31, 1517, Luther nailed 95 theses against the Church in Wittenberg, Germany. Four years later, on April 18, 1521, he stood before the Diet of Worms to defend himself. If he did not recant, more than likely, he would be burned at the stake. Luther stood with boldness and clarity of thought. After giving his speech in German, the Catholic leaders wanted him to give a simple answer of recant or no recant in Latin.

The end of Luther's answer went like is: "If, then, I am not convinced by proof from Holy Scripture, or by cogent reasons, if I am not satisfied by the very text I have cited, and if my judgment is not in this way brought into subjection to God's word, I neither can nor will retract anything; for it cannot be either safe or honest for a Christian to speak against his conscience. Here I stand. I cannot do otherwise. God help me. Amen." The people listening to Paul were moved much like the people listening to Luther. While some believed, others did not. Our greatest impact is not how many people respond to the gospel but how willing we are to stand up for Christ when others want to shut Him down. Jesus Christ saves, and we share.

Read Acts 26:1-32   Date: _____

GRASP
BIBLE JOURNAL PERSONAL NOTES

G   What **Grabbed** your attention, confused you or stood out?

R   What did you **Realize** about God and the people in this passage?

God?

People?

A   How could you **Apply** this to your life?

> *Is there a sin to avoid?*
> *Is there a command to obey?*
> *Is there a promise to claim?*
> *Is there an example to follow?*
> *Is there a truth to know?*

S   What is one **Specific** thing you could do this week to apply the truth from this passage? Write out "I will…".

P   Write a **Prayer** of commitment to the Lord.

What are you **Thankful** for today?

Write out a verse from this chapter to **Memorize** this week:

"Be sure you put your feet in the right place, and then stand firm."
~ *Abraham Lincoln*

27

Acts 27:1-44

No Storm is too Strong

When you read this chapter, you might think about the movies *The Perfect Storm* or *Titanic*. Luke's account is so vivid that you feel you are actually on the boat or at least watching this like it was a movie. The detail keeps you enthralled but also verifies the historicity of Luke's account. You can only imagine how Dr. Luke, wired for detail as a physician, had been paying attention to every movement on the ship. His account is truly one of the best accounts of a ship under stress and the decisions for survival that must be made in critical moments.

Under the smoothest conditions for sailing, it would have taken them five weeks to get from Caesarea to Rome. By the time the trip was over, they had been on this journey for well over four months. Paul had warned them at the beginning that things were not going to go well. The sailors must have laughed at Paul when they started with a good wind pushing them along. However, it wasn't long before they wished they had listened to Paul. A strong nor'easter, nicknamed "Eurakylon," a Greek and Latin combination of east and north winds, blew down from the North as they sailed below Crete. Thinking of Jonah yet? The sailors threw everything overboard, no one ate (who could?), and they all feared for their lives ... except for one man on board: Paul.

As if he was in a synagogue reasoning with the Jews about the Gospel or standing at the Areopagus on Mar's Hill, Paul began to share the word of God with them (27:21-26). God had told Paul that he must go to Rome, so Paul slept like a baby every night, knowing that God was in control. You should never doubt that God is in control of your life moment by moment. Just as Jesus slept on board the ship during the storm (Luke 8:22-25), you can put aside your anxiety and rest, knowing that He is the One who calms the storms and rides through them with you.

You are never outside the presence of God. His Spirit lives within you, and He will NEVER leave you or forsake you, no matter how strong the storms of life are! When Paul stood to speak to the sailors and prisoners in that critical moment, he was not Paul the proclaimer of the Gospel, but an ordinary man among ordinary men, a prisoner of Rome. However, Paul took charge as a leader. John Stott commented, "It was more than mature experience at sea which made Paul stand out as a leader on board ship; it was his steadfast Christian faith and character." Leaders always rise from positions of purpose and character.

The most critical part of the story comes when Paul tells them all to stay on the ship, "Unless the men stay in the ship, you cannot be saved." The ship, at that moment, was like Noah's Ark. Outside the ship was only death, but inside the ship was safety. Life is like this. In Christ, there is safety, protection, and life, but outside of Christ, there is death and hopelessness. Thankfully, we don't have to hold on to the sails, because Christ is holding on to us. We are safe in Him!

Read Acts 27:1-44   Date: _____

GRASP

BIBLE JOURNAL PERSONAL NOTES

G   What **Grabbed** your attention, confused you or stood out?

R   What did you **Realize** about God and the people in this passage?

God?

People?

A   How could you **Apply** this to your life?

> Is there a sin to avoid?
> Is there a command to obey?
> Is there a promise to claim?
> Is there an example to follow?
> Is there a truth to know?

S   What is one **Specific** thing you could do this week to apply the truth from this passage? Write out "I will…".

P   Write a **Prayer** of commitment to the Lord.

What are you **Thankful** for today?

Write out a verse from this chapter to **Memorize** this week:

"Storms always point to a God greater than ourselves."
~ Anonymous

28

Acts 28:1-31

The Rest of the Story

Paul Harvey was a radio personality from 1951 to 2008, reaching as many as 24 million people during his programs. His most famous tagline is known by so many and used when wanting to tell: "The Rest of the Story." When you look at the end of Acts, you want Paul Harvey to say, "And now, the rest of the story", but Luke doesn't really do this. When we watch movies or read books, we expect a satisfying ending that ties everything together. We understand if we know a sequel is coming, but Acts seems to end abruptly. There are no loose ends tied up or untold stories that get a clean finale. You can get to the end of Acts and think, "Wait! What? Does Paul stand before Caesar? Does he ever go on beyond Rome to Spain? Did he get out of his chains to continue preaching? What happened?" It might surprise you what Luke could have been up to here. Paul and the crew had beached the ship on the island of Malta.

Luke graciously records that the people were unusually kind. That's always a bonus when we come into a strange area. Immediately, Paul is believed to be evil because of a snake bite. However, when he shook off the snake and didn't swell up or die, they believed him to be a god. The story shifts to a man named Publius, whom God used to provide them hospitality and through whom the gospel was shared through a miracle with Publius's father. After their three-month stay, they sailed for Rome.

Finally, they are in the place God had told Paul he would go, surrounded by believers who were thrilled that Paul was in their city and, once again, faced with defending himself before the Jewish leaders. During these days, Paul was constantly sharing the gospel, expounding the scriptures (Nehemiah 8:8), and seeing new converts come to faith in Jesus Christ. The restrictions on Paul seemingly lessened; he could move freely from house to house.

Merida points out that, during these days in Rome, that Paul's mindset was about ministry, even while in prison: "Continue steadfastly in prayer, being watchful in it with thanksgiving. At the same time, pray also for us, that God may open to us a door for the word, to declare the mystery of Christ, on account of which I am in prison – that I may make it clear, which is how I ought to speak. Walk in wisdom toward outsiders, making the best use of the time. Let your speech always be gracious, seasoned with salt, so that you may know how you ought to answer each person" (Col. 4:2-6).

This was the life of Paul and all those ministering with him. Look at what he said in Colossians 4. He did not ask them to pray for him to be released but that more opportunities come to share the gospel. We are so prone to want to get out of a bad situation that we don't realize that within such conditions, there are opportunities for ministry!

So, how would Paul Harvey share "the rest of the story?" The fact is, YOU are the rest of the story. Luke ends it with the gospel going forth, but throughout church history, the story has continued, and now we are the ones to keep the story moving forward! We are the ones who continue to write the history of the witness of Christ to every nation. To God be the glory!

Read Acts 28:1-31   Date: _____

GRASP
BIBLE JOURNAL PERSONAL NOTES

G What **Grabbed** your attention, confused you or stood out?

R What did you **Realize** about God and the people in this passage?

God?

People?

A How could you **Apply** this to your life?

> *Is there a sin to avoid?*
> *Is there a command to obey?*
> *Is there a promise to claim?*
> *Is there an example to follow?*
> *Is there a truth to know?*

S What is one **Specific** thing you could do this week to apply the truth from this passage? Write out "I will…".

P Write a **Prayer** of commitment to the Lord.

What are you **Thankful** for today?

Write out a verse from this chapter to **Memorize** this week:

"If you don't live it, you don't believe it."

~ Paul Harvey

References

1. Keller, Timothy. *Spiritual Friendship*, Sermon excerpt from a series, The Church: How to Believe Despite Christians, www.gospelinlife.org, March 1, 1998.

2. Harvey, Paul. www.paulharveyarchives.com

3. Ironside, H.A. *Acts*, Loizeaux Brothers, Neptune, New Jersey, 1998.

4. Stott, John R.W. *The Message of Acts: The Spirit, the Church and the World*, Intervarsity Press, 1990.

5. Merida, Tony. *Christ-Centered Exposition of Acts*, Holman Reference, Nashville, Tennessee, 2017.

6. Bruce, F.F. *The Book of Acts*, William B. Eerdmans Publishing, Grand Rapids, Michigan, 1988.

7. Phillips, John. Exploring Acts, Loizeaux Brothers, Neptune, New Jersey, 1986.

8. Stories and Anecdotes were sourced through www.sermoncentral.com and www.sermonillustrations.com

9. Quotes included in this devotional were sourced through www.goodreads.com

10. Conzelmann, Hans. *A Commentary on the Acts of the Apostles*, Philadelphia Fortress Press, 1987, p. xxxiii.

11. Anonymous Commentary from Writers at Blue Letter Bible, www.blueletterbible.org

About the Author

Dr. Craig Hamlin lives in Newnan, Georgia, with his wife and daughter. He earned a Doctor of Ministry in Expository Preaching from Southeastern Baptist Theological and currently serves a local church in the Atlanta area. Craig enjoys woodworking, speaking, writing, leading, and teaching around the world. He has taught in Japan, the Philippines, Romania, Hungary, Ukraine, Israel, and Greece.

Made in the USA
Columbia, SC
04 July 2023